The Soviet Union
and the
Emerging Nations

Also by Harish Kapur

SOVIET RUSSIA AND ASIA 1917–1927

The Soviet Union
and the
Emerging Nations

A CASE STUDY OF SOVIET POLICY
TOWARDS INDIA

Harish Kapur

Professor in International Relations
Graduate Institute of International Studies, Geneva

Published by Michael Joseph Ltd
for the Graduate Institute of International Studies, Geneva

First published in Great Britain by
MICHAEL JOSEPH LIMITED
52 Bedford Square
London, W.C.1
for the Graduate Institute of International Studies, Geneva, 1972

© *1972 by the Graduate Institute of International Studies, Geneva*

(7181 0961 9)

Set and printed in Great Britain by
Unwin Brothers Limited at the Gresham Press, Woking,
in Bembo type, twelve-point leaded, and bound by
James Burn at Esher, Surrey

CONTENTS

PREFACE

Between the two World Wars, Europe occupied prime place in Soviet diplomacy. It was towards Europe that the Bolshevik leaders turned to in order to encourage Communist revolutions; and it was in this part of the world that they principally concentrated their diplomatic activities, once it became apparent that Communist revolutions did not seem possible. In fact, so overwhelmingly important was this factor in Soviet operational diplomacy that one could venture to suggest that Moscow's policy towards Asia was often determined by its requirements in Europe. A hardening of its policy in Europe, for example, invariably led to the embarkation of revolutionary offensives in Asia, a shift to a policy of moderation often culminated in the formulation of a soft line towards the Asian colonies. Even when Moscow turned to Asia with deep interest— as was the case in the early twenties—it had apparently done so with the primary aim of creating revolutionary situations in Europe by putting its rear in jeopardy.

However, after World War II a new orientation became evident in Soviet policy. While interest in Europe continued to rise due to sizable Soviet involvement in Eastern Europe, one also began to witness a collateral upsurge in Soviet interest in Asia. Apparently the emerging continent had come of age and consequently needed, according to the new Soviet thinking, to be treated as an independent factor unconnected and uninfluenced by Soviet requirements in Europe.

What are the reasons for this new Soviet orientation? How come that within the span of a decade after World War II, the Asian continent has come to acquire such an important position in Soviet thinking and operational diplomacy? Was it because, in the morrow of Russia's greatest victory, she had emerged as a super-power with clear-cut determination to consider—like the United States—the entire globe as a chessboard on which cautious moves had to be made? Or was it because a lack of interest in Asia on the part of Moscow, after the Chinese Communist revolution in 1949, would have been tantamount to the abdication of hegemony to the Communist Party of China which had already moved to arrogate to itself the leadership of Asian revolutions? Whatever may have been the reasons, the detailed examinations of which would

7

lead us beyond the scope of this short preface, one thing is certain: Soviet involvement in Asia had indeed become sizable.

Within the general framework of this interest, there were obviously some countries in the region which, by the very nature of their size, population, political orientation and natural resources, were considered as principal targets of Soviet diplomacy. India naturally was one of them. Apart from her size, massive population and strategic location, she had, within a few years, acquired an important status in the world whose role and influence in international affairs had, in some ways, become decisive.

A case study of Soviet policy towards India is therefore vital; for it should permit a scholar to draw some general, though tentative, conclusions about some of the basic factors that determine Soviet diplomatic behaviour. An effort has thus been made in this short study to analyse the evolution of Indo-Soviet relations, the factors that influenced Soviet policy and the different motivations that have determined Soviet thinking towards India. But this is not an attempt to analyse exclusively Soviet policy towards India; for the foreign policy of no nation is formulated in a vacuum, and the diplomatic initiatives of no nation are completely un-influenced by the actions of others. For example, it is hardly possible to understand the different fluctuations in Soviet policy towards India without closely examining the actions and reactions of the nations that constitute the Asian sub-system.

In the preparation of this study, I have received so much generous support from so many friends in India and elsewhere that it is quite impossible here to acknowledge individually my debts and gratitude. I must however express my thanks to Jacques Freymond, the Director of the Graduate Institute of International Studies in Geneva, for his continuous and thoughtful encouragement and to the Rockefeller Foundation for a generous grant which enabled me to travel to India in 1968 to discuss with public and academic figures the different facets of Indo-Soviet relations.

Chapter I

THE HISTORIC FRAMEWORK

Soviet Policy in Asia

From the voluminous literature that is now available, it is evident that the Soviet leaders have displayed a continuous doctrinal interest in Asia since the Bolshevik Revolution. From an ideology originally relevant to the developed European societies, they have, through the years, transformed Marxism into a revolutionary strategy applicable to countries far removed from the preliminary stage of industrialization. From a theoretical concept aimed at radical distribution of the already produced wealth, it has been converted into a movement aiming at the creation of wealth through the coercive power of the state. And from a doctrine that was to inspire revolutions in Europe, it has gradually evolved into a concept that inextricably linked the consummation of revolutions in Europe with their success in Asia.

But, despite the constant manifestation of doctrinal interest in Asia, Europe, during the first two years after the October revolution, was none the less the principal preoccupation of Soviet operational diplomacy. It was towards Europe that the Bolshevik leaders first turned in order to encourage Communist revolutions; and it was in this part of the world that they primarily concentrated their offensive-defensive diplomatic actions once it became increasingly evident that revolutions did not seem possible.

This initial concentration on the European continent was dictated by a number of objective factors: in the first place, Communist revolutions in Europe were believed to be around the corner. Many countries in the area were seething with discontent. In the immediate aftermath of World War I, practically everywhere one witnessed the phenomena of upheavals, discontent, economic dislocation, etc. And in more than one country—but particularly in Germany—revolutionary organizations were set up, workers organized and strikes launched to bring down what appeared to many to be the crumbling social, political and economic structures.

The Bolshevik leaders, therefore, considered their own revolution only as a prelude to the explosion of a series of revolutions that would engulf the continent and would eventually culminate in the communization of at least a few countries.[1]

This assessment of the European situation compounded with the general revolutionary mood that was discernible among the Soviet leaders generated a haughty contempt for the traditional conceptions of diplomacy, and encouraged them to take the necessary steps to accelerate the revolutionary process. Trotsky, who was the first Commissar of Foreign Affairs, made it clear that he had no need for diplomacy, and Lenin, even a few weeks before the October revolution, considered that 'the international situation gives us a series of objective grounds for believing that if we came out now, we shall have all proletarian Europe on our side'.[2]

Bolshevik Russia's geographic position was the second factor that contributed to the lack of any operational interest in Asia. The region directly under Soviet influence was separated from the Asian countries by wide areas in Central Asia, Trans-Caspia, Trans-Caucasia and Siberia who had either declared their independence from Moscow or were under the control of 'White' generals. Thus when the Soviet leaders spoke about Asia, they usually referred to those areas which hitherto constituted a part of the Russian empire rather than countries over which Russia had hardly ever exercised any effective control. That this was understandable is evident from the fact that the Soviet leaders could hardly pursue a viable foreign policy as long as they were separated from Asia by wide territories controlled by anti-Soviet forces.

Thirdly, the Soviet leaders did not look to Europe only with expectancy and hope. They also dreaded the undermining of their own revolution through attacks originating from capitalist Europe. Such a fear was perhaps not unfounded; for many responsible European leaders had publicly manifested their displeasure at the developments in Russia, and some had even announced their intention to undermine the revolutionary government before it acquired all the characteristic features of a stable régime. In fact, an effort to this effect was made during 1918–20 by the Allied powers when troops belonging to some of them landed in different parts of Soviet territory. Evidently this military initiative did not succeed

[1] A few pages of this chapter are either reproduced or based on author's *Soviet Russia and Asia 1917–27. A Study of Soviet Policy towards Turkey, Iran and Afghanistan* (London: 1960).

[2] Cited in E. H. Carr, *The Bolshevik Revolution, 1917–1923*, Vol. 3 (London: 1966), p. 20.

as it was half-hearted and consisted merely of a series of confused and uncoordinated military actions which lacked any centralized planning. But it was obvious that had the Allied powers really shown determination in their intervention efforts, had they successfully co-ordinated their plans, it would have been possible for them—with their superior power—to undermine the Russian Revolution.

By 1920, however, the general situation in Soviet Russia as well as Europe had undergone a significant permutation, leading to the dilation of Bolshevik interest in Asia. With the defeat of Kolchak and Denikin, it became possible slowly to bring under Soviet control the eastern border-lands which had declared their independence immediately after the October Revolution. Soviet Russia now found herself contiguous to such Asian states as Iran, Turkey, Afghanistan and China; and it was conse-quently no longer possible for the Bolshevik leaders to take only a theoretical interest in Asia or simply issue appeals to the Asian people to revolt against their internal and external oppressors. Obviously, some-thing more was needed to draw the revolutionary masses of the Asian nations into an alliance with the revolutionary workers and peasants of Soviet Russia.

In addition, the Communist revolutions in Europe, on which so much hope had been placed, had not succeeded. The revolutionary uprising, staged by Communists in Berlin in January 1919, not only failed to ignite an October Revolution, but ended in disastrous defeat and physical elimination of Rosa Luxemberg and Karl Liebknecht, the two outstanding leaders of German Communism. The Munich Soviet collapsed after a few weeks, and the Hungarian Soviet Government quickly disintegrated under heavy internal and external pressures. Hope again flickered in the summer of 1920, when the Red Army stood at the gates of Warsaw; but this did not last long because the Poles launched a counter-attack that led to the general withdrawal of the Soviet Army and, along with it, the virtual disappearance of all hope of successful revolutions in Europe.

The Asian continent, on the other hand, was seething with discontent. Almost all the countries were undergoing profound revolutionary changes in the early twenties. Under Amanullah, Afghanistan had become inde-pendent. The Turkish nationalist movement, under Kemal Pasha, had transformed itself into a viable government; and the Iranian régime was fast becoming independent of British control. In China, waves of mass protest against Japan had been launched by students. Working-class movements had gained momentum in Shanghai, Hankow and elsewhere.

General unrest among workers and peasants in India culminated in a series of large-scale political and economic strikes. And, even more important for revolutionary Russia, the year 1920–21 witnessed the formation of Communist parties of Iran, Indonesia and China.

All these momentous upheavals did not fail to impress the Bolshevik leaders. If Europe had failed them, Asia could revive their flagging spirits. Lenin, who had rapidly grasped the importance of these events, did not hesitate to express his satisfaction over the manner in which Asia was rapidly changing. In almost all his communications and reports, during the first few months of 1920, he pointedly referred to Asia. At the All-Russian Central Executive Committee meeting, held on 2 February 1920, he spoke confidently of the importance of 'our relations with the peoples of the East'.[1] In an interview with the *New York Evening Journal* on 21 February, he underlined the awakening of the eastern people 'to a new life, a life without exploitation, without landlords, without capitalists, without merchants';[2] and in still another report, delivered to the All-Russian Congress of Toiling Cossacks on 1 March, he stressed that in almost every Asian country there was 'an awakening of political consciousness, and the revolutionary movements grow from day to day'.[3]

(a) *New strategy for Asia*

Having made this initial shift, the question with which the Bolshevik leaders were then confronted was what policy should they formulate, what concrete strategy should they follow in order to draw the Asian masses into an alliance with the workers and peasants of Russia? A simple declaration that Asia had become a significant factor was not enough. Obviously a new policy was needed, and a new strategy and tactics were required.

It was to these tasks that the Soviet leaders then turned their attention. The whole issue was extensively discussed at the Second Congress of the Comintern in July–August 1920,[4] and found its characteristic expression

---

[1] V. I. Lenin, *The National Liberation Movement in the East* (Moscow: 1957), p. 238.

[2] *Ibid.*, p. 240.

[3] *Ibid.*, p. 244.

[4] For an interesting account of the national-colonial question discussed at the second congress of the Comintern, see M. N. Roy, *M. N. Roy Memoirs* (Bombay: 1964), pp. 368–82.

at the Baku Congress in September of the same year[1] and at the first congress of the Toilers of the Far East in January 1922.[2]

When the national and the colonial question came up for discussion at the second Comintern congress, it soon became clear that, although the general theme of the liberation of the oppressed people through a world-wide proletariat revolution was acceptable to all, serious differences existed concerning the role of the national bourgeoisie in the national liberation movements and the type of relations Asian Communist parties should foster with them.

Two sets of theses on the question were presented respectively by Lenin and M. N. Roy, a young Indian revolutionary. Proceeding from the basic assumption that the Asian countries were going through bourgeois democratic revolutions, Lenin proposed that it was the duty of the Communist parties to assist such revolutions and even enter into alliance with them. But, he insisted, this support and alliance should be temporary and on the condition that 'the elements of future proletarian parties, which will be Communist not only in name, are brought together and trained to understand their special tasks, i.e. those of the struggle against the bourgeois democratic movements within their own nations'.[3] There was an obvious implication in his thesis that the bourgeoisie in the colonial countries was essentially progressive.

M. N. Roy, on the other hand, argued that the bourgeoisie in the dependent areas was essentially reactionary in character, and would not perform the task which had been assigned to it by history. Consequently, the foremost objective was to set up Asian Communist parties which would organize the peasants and workers and lead them on to Communist revolutions. He maintained that the bourgeoisie, even in such advanced colonial countries as India, was not economically and culturally different from the existing social order and 'therefore the nationalist movement was ideologically reactionary in the sense that its triumph would not mean a bourgeois democratic revolution'.[4]

There does not seem to be any doubt that Roy's Indian background and his assessment of the Indian independence movement had clearly shaped

---

[1] For details see *Pervyi s'ezd narodnovo Vostoka: Baku 1–8 sentiabria 1920. Stengraficheski otchet* (Moscow: 1920).

[2] For details see *The First Congress of the Toilers of the Far East held in Moscow January 21– February 1, 1922: Closing session in Petrograd February 2, 1922* (Petrograd: 1922).

[3] V. I. Lenin, 'Draft Thesis on the National-Colonial Question', *Collected Works*, Vol. 31 (Moscow: 1966), p. 150.

[4] M. N. Roy, *op. cit.*, p. 379.

his concept of the Asian class struggle. An important basis of his distrust of the bourgeoisie, for example, seems to have emerged from his perception of a significant shift in British policies and his realization that the Indian bourgeoisie had favourably responded to the shift. During World War I, Great Britain, unable to keep Indian markets supplied with manufactured goods, reversed her traditional policy of keeping India industrially backward, thus bringing the Indian bourgeoisie into her confidence and presenting the Indian capital with a free field of development. The British Government in 1916 had even gone to the length of appointing an Indian Industrial Commission in order to encourage the installation of industries in the country. Consequently, by the end of the war, the Indian capitalist class had achieved such economic security that the government could no longer ignore the demands of political reforms and in due course largely met them by the Montague–Chelmsford reforms.[1] The idea behind this remarkable change, according to Roy, was to split the revolutionary movement by making it clear to the bourgeoisie that it was possible to realize the latter's ambitions under British rule. Although from time to time Roy revised his assessment of the bourgeois relationship with the British and Indian masses, the main theme of his argument, however, did not change.

Both of the theses were extensively discussed at the Commission which had been specially appointed to consider the national and colonial question. According to Roy, Lenin made it clear in the Commission as well as in private meetings with him, that the national liberation movements had the significance of bourgeois democratic revolution, that each stage of social revolution being historically determined, the dependent countries must have their bourgeois revolutions before they entered the stage of proletarian revolution.[2] The role of Gandhi, states Roy, was the crucial point of difference. Lenin believed that as the inspirer and leader of mass movement, Gandhi was revolutionary, while Roy insisted that a religious and culturalist revivalist like Gandhi was bound to be reactionary socially, however revolutionary he might appear politically.[3]

Lenin's thesis emerged from the Commission with a number of amendments, the most important of which was the replacing of the word 'bourgeois democratic' by 'national revolutionary', which undoubtedly applied to bourgeois democratic revolution, but obviously had a more

---

[1] The special feature of the Montague–Chelmsford reforms was the devolution of authority to the provinces, thus paving the way for federalism, the introduction of ministerial responsibility in the provinces and the system of dyarchy.

[2] M. N. Roy, op. cit., p. 379.   [3] Ibid.

revolutionary sound. While explaining the revised draft to the plenary session, he clearly stated that the aforementioned revision did not really change the thesis as the task for the national revolutionary movement 'can only be a bourgeois democratic revolution'.[1]

Finally, after considerable debate, the second Congress sought to resolve the disagreement by approving both the theses. But despite the creation of this impression that a compromise was reached, there does not seem to be any doubt that Lenin's thinking henceforth became the sole basis of Soviet theory and practice on the national and colonial question. Roy's supplementary thesis was quickly forgotten.

Besides the left-wing group led by Roy, there was also a right-wing in the Comintern as well as in the Soviet Communist Party, which held views different from those of Lenin on the whole problem of nationalism. This group was led by Sultan-Galiev. In a series of articles in the *Zhizn Natsionalnostei* in the autumn of 1919, Galiev expressed the view that the Communist leadership had committed a great strategic blunder by placing the main emphasis on revolutionary activity in Europe.[2] The weakest link, according to him, was not the West, but the East, and the failure of Communist revolutions in other countries was primarily due to the inadequacy of Soviet efforts in the eastern world.[3] Sultan-Galiev was of the view that the eastern societies, because of their unique social, cultural and religious characteristics, required different revolutionary methods from those used in the West.[4] He therefore put forward the interesting thesis that since the bourgeoisie in the dependent areas was leading the national liberation movements, it should be the objective of the Communist parties to support them and establish lasting ties with them.

This school of thought maintained that 'since the national liberation movements in the East are specially led by the merchant bourgeoisie and the progressive clergy, it is necessary that the proletarian communists support all these revolutionary national movements whatever be their form of government and the immediate objectives of these movements'.[5] Sultan-Galiev also put forward the thesis that the Moslem people were not divided into rival social classes and that it was therefore important to

[1] V. I. Lenin, 'Report of the Commission on the National and Colonial Question—July 26', *Collected Works*, Vol. 31 (Moscow: 1966), p. 241.

[2] Sultan-Galiev, who was the editor of *Zhizn Natsionalnostei*, was in the early twenties perhaps the most important Moslem in the Soviet hierarchy; for an interesting account of his life and views, see Alexandre Bennigsen and Chantal Quelquejay, *Les Mouvements Nationaux chez les Musulmans de Russie* (Paris: 1960).

[3] *Zhizn Natsionalnostei* (5 October, 12 October and 2 November 1919).   [4] *Ibid.*

[5] Cited by Bennigsen and Quelquejay, *op. cit.*, p. 135.

B

adapt Marxist theory to the peculiar conditions of the Asian people in general and the Islamic people in particular.

Such views were openly expressed by Ryskulov and Narbuta Bekov, two of Sultan-Galiev's important followers, at Baku. Ryskulov, who was the delegate from Kazan, stressed the role of the radical bourgeoisie, which, according to him, represented the movement of independence and social revolution. He said:

We cannot expect to have exclusively a communist revolution in the East. It will have national and *petit* bourgeois character but will definitely evolve into a social movement—and since the revolutionary organization of workers is still weak, the *petit* bourgeois democrats will assume the direction.[1]

Besides insisting on the national character of revolutions in the Asian countries which would be led by the bourgeoisie, the followers of Sultan-Galiev underlined the various factors that separated the East from the West and the importance of adapting Communism to the social and cultural framework of the colonial countries. They seemed to suggest that the European Communists did not understand the colonial countries, and it was therefore important that responsibility for leading Communist movements there ought to be given to the Tartar Communists.[2]

The Comintern delegates to the Baku Congress vehemently rejected Sultan-Galiev's views and reiterated the vital necessity of establishing close collaboration between the workers of the West and the peasants of the East. But instead of countering this argument of the Moslem Communists by underlining the original line formally agreed upon at the second congress of the Comintern, they went beyond it and actually launched the Royist thesis of proletarian revolution in dependent areas. In his opening speech, Zinoviev argued in favour of creating Soviets even 'in countries where there are no town workers'.[3] Pavlovich expressed the view that all the landlords and the wealthy classes in the dependent areas 'were supporting the rule of the foreign capitalists of the international bourgeoisie'[4] and that war in these areas must be waged on two fronts, namely, against foreign capital and against the native bourgeoisie.

The thesis that was finally adopted at the congress thus openly favoured the creation of Soviets in the dependent areas. Clearly this line was in

---

[1] Cited by Bennigsen and Quelquejay, *op. cit.*, p. 136.   [2] *Ibid.*
[3] *Pervyi Sezd Narodovo Baku, op. cit.*, pp. 69–72.   [4] *Ibid.*, pp. 149–50.

direct contradiction with the thesis adopted at the second congress of the Comintern, and there are some indications that the Soviet leadership did not accept it. According to Roy, Lenin in fact criticized Zinoviev for having 'painted nationalism red'[1] and the Soviet newspapers seemed generally to have ignored all that was said in Baku.[2]

There does not seem to be any doubt that Lenin was determined to continue the relatively moderate line formulated at the second congress. Therefore, in the actual formulation of Soviet policy, the Baku congress and all that was said there played an insignificant role. In fact, one can go to the extent of stating that the congress of the Peoples of the East was nothing but a passing, though undoubtedly important, episode in Soviet history.

(b) Soviet policy during the inter-war years

Having reasserted the Leninist thesis, the Soviet leaders were now faced with the delicate and rather difficult task of applying these general theoretical formulations to the concrete reality of Asia. But before they could do so, they had to examine the different political forces operating in Asia and analyse their objectives and their orientations. Obviously it was a difficult task in view of the fact that most of the Asian countries were at different stages of political struggle and were led by nationalist leaders with different background and diverse objectives. There was Kemal Pasha in Turkey, Reza Khan in Iran, Amanullah in Afghanistan and Sun yat-sen in China, who had, in their different manners, raised the flag of nationalistic revolt against the West and who had, at the same time, either set up independent governments of their own or taken over the already existing ones. In short, the above-mentioned Asian leaders were exercising regular governmental functions with the exception that they had not completely consolidated their position in their respective countries, either because of the existence of dilapidated parallel governments or because of the influence of some outside force.

Also falling into this category of independent states were Japan and Outer Mongolia. But both of them were different from the other Asian states mentioned above and were, at the same time, also different from each other: economically Japan was as developed as any advanced European country with an imperialistic policy of her own, while under-

[1] M. N. Roy, *op. cit.*, p. 395.
[2] Ivor Spector, *The Soviet Union and the Muslim World, 1917–1958* (Seattle: 1959), p. 59.

developed Mongolia was unique in that she had, right from the beginning, hinged her fate to Soviet Russia.

Lastly, there was the rest of Asia still colonial and still far removed from the goal of independence. But the nationalist resurgence in these countries was none the less rapidly asserting itself. Everywhere peoples were rising to rid themselves of imperial domination. In Morocco, Abd-el-krim challenged the Spanish and the French; in Egypt, Soad Zoghlul Pasha led the nationalists against the British; and in Syria, there was a serious rebellion to throw off the French mandatory rule. It was perhaps in India that the nationalist movement was becoming most assertive. The rising demands of the Indian nationalists, coming increasingly under Gandhi's spell, went far beyond what the British were prepared to grant, and the Congress widened its base to become a mass movement capable of virtually paralysing the government.

Such was thus the type of Asia that confronted the Soviet leaders when they set their sights on that continent. From the various statements and declarations made by the Soviet leaders,[1] it would appear that there was a general consensus of opinion in Moscow that the nationalist governments in Afghanistan, Turkey, China and Iran were revolutionary and, as such, worthy of Soviet support.

With regard to the rest of Asia, Soviet policy was relatively straightforward. It was, as we shall see below, concerned with the basic objective of assisting these countries to become independent. So in effect there were two different types of Soviet policies in Asia: one—which could be characterized as diplomatic—was directed towards countries which had already attained their political independence, and the other—revolutionary —applicable to the colonial areas which were still far removed from the goal of national independence.

Towards the independent nations of Asia, the main thrust of Soviet policy during the entire inter-war period was to seek collaboration with nationalist governments and to extend Soviet influence over them by gradual and unobtrusive methods, without of course undermining the opportunities for profitable economic relations with western countries. Military, political and economic assistance was given to the governments of Kemal Ataturk in Turkey, Sun yat-sen in China, Amanullah in

---

[1] There is no one consolidated Soviet declaration or article of this period in which it has been clearly stated that these countries are revolutionary and therefore ought to be supported. There are a number of different writings in which views to this effect have been expressed. For details, see V. I. Lenin, *National Liberation Movement in the East* (Moscow: 1957).

Afghanistan, in order to bring about the decimation of western influence; and no stone was left unturned—including military and diplomatic threats—to persuade the Iranian Government to loosen its political and economic ties with Great Britain.

Towards the colonial world, the Soviet policy was frankly revolutionary. Despite many tactical fluctuations, Moscow's basic and permanent objective was to extend open support, both moral and material, to nationalistic forces seeking independence from European control. This policy was unfettered by the confines and trappings of traditional diplomacy, for these countries were not independent states with whom diplomatic relations could be established. There were no national governments with whom the Soviet leadership would establish political or economic relations. There was no question of signing treaties of friendship, alliance or non-aggression with such countries. What the Soviet leaders had to deal with in the colonial areas was the rising opposition of political forces seeking power to establish governments that would be nationalistic in their objectives, policies and outlooks.

Within the framework of such a policy, India was considered as an important factor which merited considerable attention by the Soviet leaders. In fact, even when the eyes of the Bolshevik leaders were concentrated on revolutionary developments in Europe, India was not completely ignored. They were convinced, no less than the Tsars before them, that a threat to British power in India would seriously undermine British power all over the world. By way of India, they could weaken an enemy who represented the principal obstacle to world revolution and the most dangerous menace to the security of the Soviet Government itself. Moreover, apart from offering a weapon against Great Britain, India, in herself, presented an attractive base for the export of revolution in other Asian countries.

It is therefore not surprising that open support was often extended to the Indian nationalist movement: contacts were established with Indian revolutionaries, a military school was set up in Tashkent to train Indians;[1] even important efforts were made to create an advance base for Indian revolutionary activities in Afghanistan.[2]

There were of course myriad fluctuations in Soviet tactics and strategy during the inter-war period. There were periods when the Soviet decision-makers, having formulated a general left-wing strategy, denounced the policies of the Indian nationalist leaders and encouraged the Indian Communists to adopt an independent militant line. And there were

[1] M. N. Roy, *op. cit.*, p. 421.   [2] *Ibid.*

periods when the Soviet leaders, having formulated a general right-wing strategy, accepted the Indian National Congress leaders as genuine nationalists and encouraged a united nationalist front under their leadership. There were even periods when the imperatives of national survival—as during World War II—emboldened them to encourage the temporary abandonment of the nationalist struggle and institute collaboration with British imperialism in order to defeat Nazism.[1]

In pursuing such policies in the independent and the colonial areas of Asia, the Soviet Government was often trespassing in Great Britain's sphere of influence, and was thereby coming into conflict with the British. This was nothing new. It had already happened during the time of Tsarist Russia. In fact, the entire history of the last century was, to a considerable degree, a history of Anglo-Russian conflicts. In the Crimean War, in the Russo-Turkish wars of 1822 and 1877, in the war with the Caucasus, and finally, in all the Central Asian campaigns, Russia faced the Britain of Palmerston, Chamberlain and Curzon either as an open or secret enemy.

When the Bolsheviks came to power, this conflict became even more acute. The British could understand Tsarist Russia; for it was a country which, while an enemy, had a social and political outlook relatively approximate to their own and which could be counted on to observe the norms of traditional diplomacy. The Tsarist, in other words, having the same conceptual framework as the British, could negotiate and even bargain. The Bolsheviks were different. Their revolutionary statements were totally incomprehensible to the empire-oriented British. They were in some ways a greater menace to Britain than were their predecessors since they could not be persuaded—at least in the initial stages—into bargaining the future of Asia.

Thus the first thirty years of Bolshevik history also were times of constant and continuous conflict with Great Britain. The Bolsheviks, like the Tsarist Russian leaders, attempted to dethrone Britain from the Straits, to oust her from Iran, to neutralize her influence in Afghanistan and knock at the very doors of India where the situation had become ominous for British interests. But the similarity between the Soviet and Tsarist leaders ends here. The Tsarist leaders were driven, by the very nature of their economic and political outlook, to aim at displacing British influence in order to move into vacated areas to pursue a policy more or less similar to that of the British. The Bolsheviks, on the other

[1] For details see David N. Druhe, *Soviet Russia and Indian Communism* (New York: 1959).

hand, by the very nature of their revolutionary outlook, at least during most of the inter-war period, were driven to strengthen nationalist governments in independent countries, and to extend moral and material support to nationalist movements in countries aspiring to become independent. The first thirty years of Soviet history, so far as Asia is concerned, are thus filled with declarations, proclamations and appeals as well as revolutionary and diplomatic activities in order to effectuate the complete isolation and eventual defeat of imperialism. But despite all this support extended to nationalism, Soviet influence did not, however, increase among the Asian nationalist movements; and imperialism did not really suffer any set-backs. If anything, the colonial powers, during the inter-war period, continued to exercise effective control over areas under their domination.

How can one explain this phenomenon? Why did the Soviet Union fail to exercise an important influence over nationalist movements when she was perhaps the only major country that openly supported nationalism?

In the first place, this can be attributed to the fact that during the inter-war years, Soviet Russia, despite her geographical position both as a European and Asian country, was still a region which did not possess the necessary military and political power to undertake bold actions in areas which happened to be distant from the heart of Russia; and the heart of Russia for the Bolsheviks was situated in Europe, for it was in this area that there existed the core of her industrial and military complex. Secondly, the Soviet failure was probably due to the myriad fluctuations that were discernible in her policy towards the existing nationalist movements. There were periods when the non-Communist nationalist leaders were denounced for their 'reactionary' outlook, and the Communist parties were considered as the only viable and ideologically acceptable forces against imperialism. And there were periods when the Soviet leaders considered the nationalist forces as a progressive factor, and viewed their role as important in the history of their nations. Such conspicuous and metronomic fluctuations, which were often determined by the needs of Soviet national interests, tended partly to tarnish the Soviet image and encouraged many to question Soviet credibility on the whole issue of nationalism. Lastly, the blind and often thoughtless subservience of the Asian Communist parties must have significantly contributed to the development of prudence among the nationalist leaders. For, they who were striving for the independence of their nations, the intellectual and often financial dependence on external forces must have encouraged them to discern the non-nationalist character of Asian Communist parties.

(c) *The war years*

With the commencement of World War II, Soviet interest in Asia suffered a serious decline. In fact after Hitler's attack on the USSR in June 1941, it ceased almost entirely. No activity unrelated to the war effort was allowed. Soviet scholars including Orientalists became correspondents. The objective of world revolution was abandoned and the Comintern was dissolved. The few articles that appeared in the Soviet press concerning India, for example, completely ignored the political situation in the country and concentrated attention on the strategic war potential of India.[1] One Soviet writer went to the extent of showing himself entirely in sympathy with the British position when the latter rejected the demands of independence of Indian nationalists in August 1942. This was not the moment for Indian independence and 'the war against Fascist aggression', in his view, required the maximum mobilization of all of India's forces.[2] In fact so concerned and involved was the Soviet leadership with the important and immediate objective of winning the war that it was not prepared to rock the boat of Anglo-Soviet friendship by raising the sensitive question of British imperial policy on which Churchill was known to have very strong views. According to Eden at one of the meetings during the Teheran conference, Stalin actually applauded Churchill's eloquent defence of the British trusteeship system, to the visible embarrassment of Roosevelt who was known to be a strong partisan of Indian independence.[3]

(d) *Soviet policy after World War II*

However by 1945, Moscow's interest in Asia gradually began to revive. The termination of the war on the European front in May of that year made it possible for Stalin to move his troops to North Korea and Manchuria. While this was in accordance with diplomatic agreements concluded with the United States and China, one cannot escape the reflection that the Soviet military presence in these areas must have brought home to the Russians the revolutionary importance of uncertain and discontented Asia. North Korea had already swung to the Soviet side,

---

[1] I. Lenin, 'Rol' Britanskoi imperii v sovermennoi voine', *Bolshevik*, No. 20 (September 1941), pp. 27–37.

[2] S. Mel'man, 'Polozhenie v Indii', *Mirovoe Khoziastvo i mirovoe politika*, No. 11–12 (November–December 1942), pp. 46–7.

[3] A. Eden, *The Reckoning* (London: 1965), p. 514.

Manchuria was infected with Chinese Communist troops, and a new government had already been set up in Tabriz, capital of Azerbaijan, under Ja'far Pishevari, a veteran Communist and Comintern agent.

None the less, while the importance of Asia was now no longer belittled, the European continent still attracted the prime attention of Soviet leaders. Considering the situation in the area, this was understandable. Almost the whole of Eastern Europe which had come under direct Soviet military control encouraged the leadership in Moscow to concentrate its principal attention in bringing the entire area under its political and economic control. At the same time, the aftermath of war had brought serious economic dislocation and political instability in Western Europe; and the Communist parties of France and Italy had become powerful factors in the political lives of their countries. The development of such a situation did not fail to generate new hopes of kindling revolutionary fires in the heart of Western Europe. But within two to three years after the war, Soviet political and military hold over Eastern Europe was firmly established. Although signs of nationalist pride and independence were still existent, Soviet power over the whole area had indeed become unchallengeable. At the same time the Soviet hope of exercising significant influence in Western Europe was dispelled. Despite the existence of mass Communist parties in France and Italy, Western Europe rapidly asserted its determination to remain non-Communist; and within a brief period of time the whole area became stable, irrevocably limiting the range of Soviet manœuvres to minor shifts in orientation in one country or another.

There was obviously a favourable constellation of factors that contributed to the stabilization process. In the first place, the multiple pressures that had slowly led to the communization of Eastern Europe induced a strong current against the withdrawal of United States troops from Western Europe. An imaginative and large financial aid programme amounting to almost thirty billion dollars was undertaken to restore political and economic stability. At the same time, Washington 'gave fair warning that, if necessary, it was prepared to meet Soviet force with American force, rather than with mere protests and resolutions in the United Nations'.[1] Secondly, the West European decision-makers displayed a remarkable determination to resist Soviet pressures and rapidly reached a consensus that co-ordinated policy and some form of unity of the non-Communist nations was the only guarantee for the effective

[1] Dean Acheson, *Present at the Creation. My Years in the State Department* (London: 1970), p. 194.

defence of their own institutions. Thirdly, the radical transformation of military technology—including the initial American monopoly of nuclear weapons—introduced an element of restraint in Soviet militancy and probably encouraged Moscow to abandon any intention it might have had of exercising pressure in Western Europe.

The situation in Asia, by contrast, was far from stable. As a result of the stresses and strains engendered by the war, almost the entire area was undergoing profound revolutionary changes. The colonial powers, greatly weakened by the turbulence of the war, were no longer in a position to reassert their authority. The Indian nationalist movement's demand for complete independence could no longer be forestalled by victorious but none the less weak Britain. The massive tide of nationalistic revolts in Indonesia, Indo-China and other countries could no longer be contained. And China was deeply riven by an escalating civil war in which the interests of the western world had been seriously compromised.

The Soviet Union could hardly ignore these developments. To have done so would have in effect meant the abdication of the hegemony to the Communist Party of China, who, though still far removed from the goal of power, was none the less slowly but steadily moving in that direction.

But this was not all. There were other reasons that led the Soviet leaders to turn to Asia: in the first place the factors that had originally encouraged Soviet interests in Europe had undergone significant evolution after World War II. Communist revolutions in the advanced countries of Europe—originally considered necessary—were no longer considered indispensable for the success of Communism in Europe. A succession of five-year plans had transformed the USSR into an advanced industrialized nation, making it possible for the Soviet leaders to proclaim their entry into the stage of 'building Communism', within their national borders. The concept that the attainment of Communism in the Soviet Union required revolutions in advanced European countries had thus gone by the board. Secondly, the Soviet Union had emerged from the war with the undisputed status of a world power, while Britain, France and Germany had been considerably weakened, and had no hope of recovering their pre-war status. Thirdly, the Soviets no longer regarded Europe with the same fear as during the inter-war period. They no longer dreaded an attack from Europe, having effectively brought almost half of Europe under their firm military and political control. At the same time, hopes of communizing Western Europe, either through indigenous revolutions or through military pressure, had been dispelled, and the Soviet Union became a firm advocate of *status quo* in Europe.

Obviously, the Soviet Union could no longer assign Asia a secondary role. It could no longer permit the objectives in Europe to determine its policy in Asia. A new assessment of the Asian scene and of Soviet response thereto had thus become necessary.

But the defeat of Japan, combined with the advance of Soviet troops in China, Iran and North Korea, highly coloured the generic Soviet view of the important political changes that were taking place in Asia. The nationalist revolutions, not being of the same dimension as the Communist revolutions, were considered to be formalistic innovations of no major significance, the main purpose of which was subtly to disguise 'the continual presence of the colonial powers'. The increasing and perhaps unexpected success of the Chinese Communists in the civil war in China was for the Soviet leaders a convincing proof that Communist revolutions were around the corner. In an elaborate article, which appeared in *Bolshevik* in December 1947, Zhukov, principal Soviet spokesman on colonial affairs, sympathetically acknowledged the success of armed struggle in China and Vietnam, and unambiguously castigated the 'so-called theory of a third force'. He characterized the concept as an 'imperialist device', the purpose of which is 'to slander the USSR by placing it on the same level with American imperialism'.[1]

If Zhukov's article in the *Bolshevik* was the first serious and systematic post-war effort to assess the Asian situation, the Southeast Asian Youth Conference held in Calcutta in 1948 was the first convenient occasion to introduce this thinking in the operational strategies of the Asian Communist parties.[2] Notwithstanding the non-controversial nature of the conference, the peaceful transfer of power in some countries was criticized, and armed resistance against the nationalist government as well as the colonial powers was endorsed as the only effective method for introducing viable revolutionary changes in Asia.

[1] *Bolshevik* (Moscow: December 1947).
[2] For details see Ruth T. McVey, *The Soviet View of Indonesian Revolution* (Cornell University—Interim Reports series: mimeographed, 1957).

CHAPTER II

SOVIET HOSTILITY

Having adopted a highly negative view of the Asian process of decolonization, it was hardly possible for the Soviet leaders to welcome the changes
in India where political power was transferred to the Indian National
Congress in 1947. What is indeed remarkable is that notwithstanding
Nehru's first declaration as Minister of External Affairs of the interim
government, that the Soviet Union was India's neighbour with whom
'we shall have to undertake many common tasks and have much to do
with each other',[1] the Soviet reaction to Indian independence was
distinctly unfriendly.

The Mountbatten plan, under which Independence was accorded to
the Indian sub-continent, was criticized, and the leadership of the Congress
party was considered to have gone over to reaction by accepting the
British terms for a political settlement.[2] E. Zhukov went even further by
suggesting that the entire leadership had capitulated to imperialism
because the big bourgeoisie feared the masses more than they feared the
British; and Nehru, who had hitherto been regarded as a progressive in
his political and economic orientation, was now accused of having moved
to the right in open collaboration with such leaders as Patel.[3] Even
Gandhi was not spared. His entire thinking was considered to be the
'basic ideological weapon of the bourgeoisie for the subjection of the
masses to their influence, and a prime brake on the awakening of the
class consciousness of the workers'.[4]

The Indian policy of non-alignment was also condemned and was
considered 'to justify a policy of collaboration with English capitalism,
a policy of establishing close contact between the Indian bourgeoisie and
English capitalism'.[5]

[1] *The Statesman* (30 September 1946).   [2] *Izvestia* (5 July 1947).
[3] E. Zhukov, 'K polozheniiu v indii', *Mirovoe Khoziastvo i mirovoe politika* (July 1947),
pp. 3–4.
[4] A. Dyakov, *Natsionalny vopros i Angliisky Imperializm v Indii* (Moscow: 1948), p. 33.
[5] E. Zhukov, *loc. cit.*, p. 4.

26

As loyal adherents of the international Communist movement and devoted friends of the Soviet Union, the Communist Party of India, who had not, during the first few months of independence, reacted unfavourably to the new government, changed its party line to fit into the new Soviet pattern. In December 1947, the Central Committee bitterly excoriated the Indian bourgeoisie and castigated the Congress party, including Nehru personally; and at the second party congress of the party, held in Calcutta in February 1948, the new line was formally proclaimed. Reiterating Zhdanov's interpretation of the international situation, the political thesis, issued at the congress, held that 'though the bourgeois leadership parade the story that independence has been won, the fact is that the freedom struggle has been betrayed and the national leadership has struck a treacherous deal behind the back of the starving people, betraying every slogan of democratic revolution'.[1] The new Secretary General, Ranadive, felt confident that time was ripe for a revolution in India; and therefore called upon the working class to initiate a programme of reckless violence and insurrection with a clear-cut aim of overthrowing the existing Indian Government. Everywhere in the country, sabotage, incendiarism, loot and murder became a daily feature of the Indian political scene. Communications were disrupted, police outposts seized, village officials manhandled and violent strikes organized.[2]

(a) India turns to the West

In the face of these entrenched external attitudes and internal pressures, it was hardly possible for the Nehru government effectively to implement its policy of non-alignment. Evidently, it was possible for the Indian decision-makers to abstain from formally joining any of the two blocs and to stay out of war, should it occur; but, however, it was not possible fruitfully to conduct a non-aligned policy as long as the international political atmosphere was not conducive to the development of friendly relations with almost all states, and as long as the principal forces operating in the world community were not prepared to recognize its usefulness. For how could India prevent war, mediate in conflicts, diminish tension and expand areas of peace without the approval of the United States and the Soviet Union? How could she assume the heavy responsi-

[1] Cited in M. R. Masani, *The Communist Party of India. A Short History* (London: 1954), p. 90.

[2] For details see Government of India, *Communist Violence in India* (New Delhi: 1950).

bility of reducing tension between blocs with a view to maintaining or to bringing about peace, when the two blocs were not prepared to accept that she should engage in such activities? The meaningful implementation of non-alignment thus does not exclusively depend upon the nation which has expressed the intention to follow such a policy; it is also contingent on other factors, the most important of which is obviously the attitude of the principal forces that constitute the bipolar world.

Consequently, the Indian decision-makers did not have any great options in the actual formulation of their foreign policy. The rigid and highly explosive international situation had deprived them of any viable leverage in their actions. Therefore, while formally continuing to adhere to a policy of non-alignment, they were reduced to a position of developing relations with those nations who were receptive to Indian overtures. That is to say they found themselves moving towards the Western nations, who, though also critical of Indian policy, were none the less prepared to forge close ties in the hope of eventually persuading the Indian leaders to ally themselves with the Atlantic community.

India's large size, her relatively developed economic and political institutions and Nehru's charismatic ability were probably considered as vital and effective elements to counterbalance the multiple pressures that emanated from Peking. There was really no other country in the area who could perform this important function. Japan was still recovering from the after-effects of a disastrous defeat, and the other countries were either too small or too mired in economic and political troubles to play a leading role in foreign affairs.

Therefore, notwithstanding the differences that subsisted between the two nations, the United States sought closer political and economic relations with India. Economic assistance was given, trade was developed and some discreet soundings were made to ascertain India's interest in replacing China as the permanent member of the Security Council of the United Nations. Nehru was officially invited to visit the United States in the autumn of 1949. Although the tangible results of his visit were not particularly striking, it was none the less an important occasion for a frank exchange of views and the mutual understanding of each other's policies.[1]

The nature of American interest in India, which slowly unfolded after the Communist revolution in China, was suggested by an article of Walter Lippmann. In a column in the *New York Herald Tribune*, he

[1] For some details about Nehru's visit, see Richard P. Stebbins, *The United States in World Affairs 1949* (New York: 1950), pp. 439–41.

asked: 'Where then shall we look for allies, now that Nationalist China, the Netherlands and France are so manifestly unable to play the role in Asia which we had supposed that they would play? That, it seems to me, is the fundamental problem which has to be resolved in order to form an American policy in Asia.'[1] And he offered the following answer: 'We would be well-advised, I think, to enter into intimate consultation with Nehru about our whole course in China and in Indonesia'.[2]

India's initial orientation to the West was also partially influenced by her close identification with political ideas emanating from that area. Notwithstanding the firmly ingrained opposition to imperialism and the existence of a general sympathy for the Soviet model of economic development, the Indian leaders were attracted, influenced and even shaped by the paradigm of political and social ideas rampant in the capitals of liberal Europe. Even the deep attraction to planning and socialism noticeable among many of them was incrusted with political liberalism, making it possible for them to communicate easily with the western nations within a generally acceptable framework.

The principal strand in Nehru's thinking, for example, was liberalism as expressed in his firm and continuous devotion to political democracy and individual freedom. To these vital issues, he remained consistently faithful, never wavering even once during his entire political career, and forever insisting on the continual necessity of their firm application to all societies. Even during the initially difficult period of post-independent India, when the Communist Party of India had raised the flag of revolt, generating some confusion in some states, he declined formally to suppress the Communist movement and thereby violate some of the fundamental principles to which he was deeply attached. His deep belief in socialism, which undoubtedly provided an important stimulus to his ideas on social and economic equality, was slowly divested of doctrinaire approach; and his credence in Marxist theory, which had originally 'lighted up many a dark corner' of his mind, was abandoned for a more pragmatic approach. While continuing to strive for a 'classless society based on co-operative effort with opportunities for all', he made it clear that 'we have to pursue peaceful methods in a democratic way'.[3]

India's military and economic dependence on the West—particularly Great Britain—was also too great to permit a meaningful and effective independence in foreign affairs. Most of the vital defence equipment emanated from Great Britain. Her trade was geared to the West, and

[1] New York Herald Tribune (10 January 1949).   [2] Ibid.
[3] Jawaharlal Nehru, Speeches 1949–53 (New Delhi: 1955), p. 103.

British shipping, banking, marine insurance and investment were powerful factors in Indian commercial life. The Indian leaders were obviously conscious of this state of dependence. But considering the myriad difficulties generated by the cold war, and the unfriendly attitude adopted by Moscow leaders, it was hardly considered expedient by the Indian decision-makers to cut off their association with the West. The gains that accrued from a policy of close relations with Britain were obviously too important to be ignored. Furthermore, for a nation like India which was committed to a policy of peaceful transition and growth, a brutal snapping of her military and economic ties with London would only have generated serious problems from which it would have been difficult to extricate.

It was thus not at all surprising to discern a pro-western orientation in India's external relations on a number of issues during the first few years after independence. One of the first decisions taken by the new and independent government was to remain in the British Commonwealth. Admittedly, the Commonwealth was an association of sovereign and independent states whose members enjoyed unhindered liberty in domestic and external affairs. By taking such a decision, India was thus not in any way jeopardizing her recently acquired sovereignty. None the less, the sovereign decision to join a restricted association of politically like-minded nations was an important litmus of general Indian orientation in a deeply divided world; for nations do not join associations with which they do not have some principled affinity.

However, this was not the only sign of India's bias for the western countries. There were other important indications. At a meeting of the Commonwealth Prime Ministers in October 1948, for example, she gave her full support to Great Britain's adherence to the West European Union under the Brussels treaty, and reached substantial agreement with London on matters of defence and international relations. For a nation which had formally announced its determination to remain disengaged from the military blocs, it was indeed odd to approve a military alliance system which reinforced bipolarity and which had been strongly denounced by the Soviet Union.

India's attitude on many controversial issues discussed at the United Nations was also more approximate to the West than the Soviet Union. She supported the American proposal to establish the Interim Committee (usually known as the little Assembly) at the 1947 meeting of the General Assembly, sided with the West on the issue of holding separate elections in South Korea, and accepted the western viewpoint on the Greek Civil War. The Indian Government also ran, with American backing, against the Ukraine for a Security Council seat in the autumn of 1947. The Soviet Republic led through a series of ballots, but was unable to obtain the necessary two-thirds majority until India finally withdrew from the race.

However, if the pro-western orientation was becoming increasingly apparent on a number of major issues, India none the less maintained a fixed anti-imperialist posture, and considered it as a foremost goal of her foreign policy. On numerous occasions, Nehru proclaimed that the colonial world must become independent and actually assured nationalists of many subjugated countries of India's moral and material support. In fact, in 1948, he went to the extent of convening an Asian conference to take concerted action against the Dutch, who were attempting to reimpose their rule in Indonesia.

Such an attitude was by no means in contradiction with India's partiality for the West in so far as the leader of the western bloc—the United States—also favoured the political independence of colonial countries. In the case of Indonesia, the United States, for example, had opposed the Dutch assertion of domestic jurisdiction, and had worked out compromises which, though weak, enabled the Security Council of the United Nations to establish a three-nation committee to work on the spot in Indonesia. In the case of former Italian colonies too, Washington made it clear that the goal of any arrangement must be political independence of these areas.

It is evident that there were none the less some differences between India and the United States on the problem of decolonization: whereas the United States showed a wide concern for the interests of the metropolitan powers and attempted to adjust them with those of the colonial areas, the Indian Government was consistently and firmly outspoken on colonialism. None the less, there were colonial issues on which India, like the United States, remained muted. The Nehru government, for example, avoided badgering the British to quit Malaya, where the political situation, in 1949, was, to say the least, explosive and where the Communist Party would have been able to seize power in the event of British withdrawal. With China and North Vietnam already Communist, with Burma in the midst of a civil war between the Communists and the national government, India probably did not wish to see another strategic nation sucked into the Communist bloc.

Thus during the first two years of her independence, India found herself in the position, on the one hand, of an anti-imperialist nation eagerly supporting the unfree nations in their struggle for independence

C

and, on the other, of establishing meaningful economic and political relations with the West to the exclusion of the Soviet Union.

(b) *Rise of Communist China*

With the communization of China, the relations between India and the Soviet Union became even more strained. For the Soviet leaders, the Communist revolution in China was only a confirmation of a long-held view regarding the potentialities of Communist revolutions in Asia. But if Moscow was impressed by the unexpected success of the Chinese revolution, it was perhaps also fearful of the important impact it could have on the other Asian Communist parties. Such a possibility could not be excluded, in view of the apparent similarities existing among the Asian nations which made the Chinese experiment more relevant to Asian conditions than the one that had taken place in the Soviet Union. The surest way for Moscow to assure its continual control and prestige among the revolutionary movements thus was to assume greater initiative and greater militancy. It is therefore not surprising that the Soviet leadership became even more critical of Nehru and his government.

The Indian Prime Minister, who was visiting the United States during the month in which the Chinese revolution had taken place, was vehemently criticized. Explaining the implication of Nehru's remarks in New York that India would support the United States in any 'defensive war', a leading Soviet writer on India, Dyakov, expressed the view that 'India was prepared to offer all her resources to the Anglo-American bloc of instigators for a further cold war'.[1] Without giving any evidence, he added:

While Nehru was negotiating in the United States, in New Delhi Sardar Patel, his Deputy, was discussing with William Slim, Chief of Imperial General Staff, concrete steps for making India a military base and for suppressing people's movement in Asia.[2]

Another Soviet observer went even further and stated that 'The vacancy left by Chiang Kai-shek is being offered to Nehru',[3] while a leading article in *Pravda* alleged that 'the repression of the national liberation and democratic movements is conducted not only by the Indian capitalists and industrialists, but it appears to be a part of the world-wide plan of Wall Street and City Street to bring India into a special base of Anglo-American imperialistic plans in the East'.[4]

[1] *Pravda* (25 November 1949).   [2] *Ibid.*
[3] *New Times* (12 October 1949), pp. 20–1.   [4] *Pravda* (25 November 1949).

For India, the dramatic events of 1949 in China were hardly a favourable sign, for they had not only skewed the Asian balance of power in favour of the Communist world but had, with the Chinese occupation of Tibet in 1950, brought a new, dynamic and rather unfriendly Communist state to the very doors of India. The buffer zone that the British had created and successfully maintained to protect the northern borders of British India now disappeared suddenly;[1] and for the first time, the Himalayan region, which had remained dormant throughout history, suddenly became a live frontier generating new strategic problems that India had never faced before.

Externally, she was now faced with a coalition—China having accepted the Soviet evaluation of India—of two neighbours whose immense power and military strength was apparent, and whose attitude towards India was by no means friendly. The Chinese characterized India's non-alignment as a camouflage, considered her still to be a semi-colony and condemned Nehru as an American imperialist running dog belonging to the 'political garbage group in Asia'.[2] Mao Tse-tung personally went to the unusual length of cabling the full support of China to the Indian Communists in their violent struggle, and expressed the hope that the day was not far off when India would certainly not 'remain long under the yoke of imperialism and its collaborators'. 'Like free China', he added, 'a free India will one day emerge in the socialist and people's democratic family; that day will end the imperialist reactionary rule in the history of mankind.'[3]

The heady wine of victory, combined with ideological militancy, obviously did not favour an attitude of moderation and reasonableness. So virulent and unremittingly hostile was China's attitude to all things non-Communist, so strong was her commitment to Marxist ideology, and so new was her experience with the outside world, that she found it virtually impossible to evaluate objectively the important process of decolonization that had irrevocably swept the Asian continent in the aftermath of World War II. The Chinese leaders considered it impossible to acquire independence under a non-Communist leadership. In formulating such an assessment, they were obviously guided by the experience of

[1] The buffer zone was created in 1904 when the British Indian Government organized a military expedition against Tibet with the fixed aim of 'forestalling any likely collusion between the Dalai Lama and Russian agents'. For details see Alastair Lamb, *The China–India Border. The Origins of the Disputed Boundaries* (London: 1964), pp. 142–7.

[2] *World Culture* (22 July 1949).

[3] For complete text of the letter see V. B. Karnik (edited), *Indian Communist Party Documents 1930–56* (Bombay: 1957), p. 48.

their own country which, under the nationalist leadership of Chiang Kai-shek, had jumped from one crisis to another, finally degenerating in a total state of helplessness and dependence on the outside world.

For any empirical observer of the Chinese scene, such a traumatic experience would be a convincing proof of the poverty of Chiang Kai-shek leadership. For the Chinese Communists, with their long and rigid training of Marxism, it was much more—it was a living example of the poverty of all non-Communist leaderships.

In the face of such a situation, the Nehru government could hardly maintain a policy of non-alignment simply by making declarations to this effect; nor could it any more bask in the glory of India's great moralistic attitude towards the problems of the world, for it had become increasingly apparent that a new look at India's foreign policy had indeed become necessary. In fact some of the Indian decision-makers had become concerned with the changed situation, and had begun to suggest rapid political and military measures to face the new danger. In a remarkably perceptive letter written to Nehru as early as 7 November 1950, and only recently made public, the Minister of the Interior, Vallabhbhai Patel, analysed the threat of this potentially dangerous situation. He wrote:

The danger from the north and north-west therefore becomes both Communist and Imperialist. While our western and north-western threats to security are still as prominent as before, a new threat has developed from the north and the north-east. Thus for the first time, India's defence has to concentrate on two fronts simultaneously. Our defence measures have so far been based on the calculations of a superiority over Pakistan. In our calculations we shall now have to reckon with Communist China in the north and the north-east—a Communist China which has definite ambitions and aims and which does not, in any way, seem friendly disposed towards us.[1]

(c) *India's response to the threat*

A new situation had thus developed. In fact what was indeed paradoxical was that the new external threat coincided with the weakening of India and the resurgence of a number of difficulties that she had not faced before. In the first place, the physical withdrawal of the British power left the country militarily weak. The strong protective hand of a major power was no longer there to pursue a forward—though undoubtedly imperialistic—policy to withstand effectively any attack from the north. Even the strongest Viceroys, throughout the British

[1] Complete text in Kuldip Nayar, *Between the Lines* (New Delhi: 1969), pp. 216–22.

period of Indian history, were not faced with the problem of having to deal with a united and well-organized China, or a militant Communist party within India backed by superpowers across the Himalayas and Pamirs. Secondly, the partition of the sub-continent into two hostile states, who did not wait long to head towards a collision course, rendered the nation weak and considerably preoccupied with defending her western frontiers.

But what could India do in the light of the new situation? An alliance with the West was not possible, in view of the forthright decision of the Nehru government to make non-alignment its article of faith. Moreover, it was evident that such a decision would only have introduced explosive extra-regional problems in the area, thereby further exacerbating the tension and conflict, making it even more difficult for the Indian leaders to surmount intractable problems facing the country.

If an open and a formal orientation in the direction of the West was difficult, an alliance with the Communist world was impossible, in view of the profound ideological and political gap that separated those who were in power in India from those who were the decision-makers in Communist countries. Furthermore, considering the belligerent mood of the Communist bloc countries, there was no guarantee—indeed it was unlikely—that such a decision would have been welcomed.

None the less, it was obvious that some new approach had become necessary so far as the Communist countries were concerned, for the monolithic unity of the bloc seemed threatening. And it was in response to this need that there arose a broad consensus among the Indian decision-makers to deploy different efforts to face the new situation.

First of all a number of political and military steps were taken to strengthen India's defences. New treaties were negotiated with the vulnerable Himalayan states of Bhutan (1949), Sikkim (1950) and Nepal (1951), underlining in different degrees the interdependence between them and India. While in the case of Sikkim the protectorate status, existing already under the British, was continued,[1] the agreement with Bhutan provided that the Himalayan kingdom would be guided by the advice of the government of India in regard to its external relations.[2] With Nepal, however, only a treaty of 'everlasting peace and friendship' was concluded.[3] But considering the strategic importance of the country,

---

[1] Government of India, *Foreign Policy of India, Texts of Documents* (New Delhi: 1958), p. 27.

[2] Cited in Shanti Prasad Varma, *Struggle for the Himalayas, A Study in Sino-Indian Relations* (Delhi: 1965), p. 24.

[3] Government of India, *op. cit.*, pp. 21–3.

Nehru made it clear in the Parliament that the Himalayas are mostly in the northern borders of India and 'we cannot allow that barrier to be penetrated because it is the principal barrier of India. Therefore, much as we appreciate the independence of Nepal, we cannot allow anything to go wrong in Nepal or permit that barrier to be crossed or weakened'.[1] In addition to linking openly the safety of India to that of Nepal, the Indian Prime Minister exercised considerable pressure on the autocratic Ranas who were ruling the country to bring themselves 'into line with the democratic forces in the world today'. For not to do so, he warned, 'is not only wrong but also unwise from the point of view of what is happening in the world today'.[2] While these warnings were being openly given, support was extended to the opposition forces who had raised the flag of revolt against the Ranas. Finally, though reluctantly, they accepted the Indian proposal for free elections in 1952 and the formation of an interim cabinet of fourteen Ministers on the basis of parity between the Ranas and the popular representatives with exiled King Tribhuvan as the head of the state.[3]

Discreet steps were also taken to improve communications throughout the mountainous tribal areas to increase the number of check posts in the middle sector, and to extend the rudiments of effective administration in the sensitive north-east frontier areas right up to the McMahon line.[4] A high-level North and North-Eastern Border Defence Committee was established in 1951 to investigate the long-term aspects of Himalayan security.

But most of these steps were primarily diplomatic, administrative and police measures, the purpose of which was to bring about a modest improvement in India's defences. All the concerted defence preparations were however studiously avoided, either because of a fear of an adverse reaction from China or because of economic reasons. It could also be argued that many Indian decision-makers, who had devoted most of their political lives to non-violent struggle against the British, perhaps did not have the background or the mental outlook—at least immediately after independence—to realize the potential danger of Chinese military presence in Tibet. In fact, within a few years after the independence of the country, the armed forces shrank rapidly in importance and national esteem even while the Indian and Pakistani armies were confronting each other in Kashmir and elsewhere. The legacy of a potentially first-class

[1] Cited in P. C. Chakravarti, *India's China Policy* (Bloomington: 1962), pp. 43–4.
[2] Jawaharlal Nehru, *op. cit.*, p. 147.
[3] For details see Girilal Jarn, *India meets China in Nepal* (Bombay: 1959), pp. 7–26.
[4] See J. Kavic, *India's Quest for Security* (California: 1967), pp. 46–61.

army passed into the hands of a series of Ministers of Defence and Commanders-in-Chief of less than top quality.

However, notwithstanding the partial strengthening of India's defences, there appeared to exist a general consensus among the Indian decision-makers that political rapprochement with the Communist world was really the only rational substitute to a military confrontation. There did not seem to exist, in their view, any other option that they could rationally decide for. India presumably was too weak to defy any big nation, and too concerned with playing a moral role in international affairs to jeopardize it by having a showdown with any one of them.

It was with this frame of mind that a diplomatic offensive was launched to seek some normalization, if not complete understanding, with the Communist countries. China, being geographically and spiritually closer to India, naturally became the first objective of Indian diplomacy. Notwithstanding the radically different economic and political systems, the Indian leadership did not allow it to act as an obstacle to the development of cordial relations between the two countries. On the contrary, the emergence of a new and relatively stable China was formally looked upon favourably, and Nehru himself characterized the new Peking government as having a sense of pride and national power. He was particularly anxious that China must not be given a feeling of isolation from the rest of the world, and every effort therefore must be made to encourage her to resume normal relations with other countries; for there is nothing, he argued, which brings out the belligerence of a nation more conspicuously than its isolation and absence of contact with other nations.

Nehru therefore obstinately maintained that the development of friendly relations between Communist China and India was of vital importance to both countries. He demanded the admission of Peking into the United Nations, insisted on the return of Formosa to the People's Republic, and declined to accept the invitation of the United States to go to San Francisco to sign the Japanese Peace Treaty, on the ground that Communist China, one of the major victims of Japanese aggression during World War II, had refused to accept the American draft treaty. Furthermore, when China intervened in the Korean War, India refused to extend her support to the United Nations resolution which condemned Peking as an aggressor. So great was Nehru's desire to seek understanding with China that even when Tibet—of vital importance to India—had been forcibly incorporated by Chinese troops in 1950, he avoided a showdown, though he did not fail to make it clear to Peking that his government did not approve such action.

Twenty years after these events, Nehru's determination to seek an understanding with China is generally considered to have been a horrendous blunder. Considering all that has happened since then and the hindsight which we have consequently acquired, it is of course possible to be struck by Nehru's shortsightedness; but it would have been certainly difficult to characterize it in such a manner in 1950 when the picture of the world was quite different. Communist China was determined to integrate Tibet into the mainland, and there was not much that India could really do to forestall this determination—apart of course from the political efforts that were in fact deployed to resolve the issue. In many ways, one cannot escape the reflection that Nehru's desire to forge closer links with China was understandable, in view of her potential force and disconcerting proximity to India. The role that he visualized for India in international affairs was such that it would have been seriously thwarted by a serious conflict with the middle kingdom. Where Nehru proved shortsighted in 1950, however, was in his disinclination to increase effectively India's military strength to face the new situation.

In any event, such a single-minded policy began to pay off; for it became increasingly evident that Peking was slowly abandoning its belligerent line. The first signs of this change became apparent during the Korean War. The Chinese attitude underwent a change when it became evident that Nehru's attitude to the conflict was by no means identical to that of the western countries. Chou En-lai paid tributes to him for his contribution to end the war,[1] and Mao Tse-tung, who personally proposed a toast at the first anniversary celebrations of the Indian Republic, spoke to the Indian Ambassador in warm terms about the Indian Prime Minister, and expressed the hope of meeting him soon in China. He also underlined the importance of developing cultural and educational exchanges between the two countries.[2]

India's refusal to sign the Japanese Peace Treaty was also warmly received by the Chinese press. The *People's Daily* editorially welcomed India's decision to reject the San Francisco treaty, and expressed the view that such an action proved 'that age was past when imperialist governments can do whatever they please'.[3] In another article, signed by a 'political observer' on the same subject, the author went even further and characterized Indian action as 'a development of utmost importance'.[4]

New Delhi was thus no longer considered tied to the apron strings of the West, and Nehru was no longer condemned as the 'running dog of

---

[1] K. M. Paanikar, *In Two Chinas. Memoirs of a Diplomat* (London: 1955), p. 123.
[2] *Ibid.*   [3] *People's China* (10 September 1951), p. 39.   [4] *Ibid.*, p. 10.

imperialism'. With great rapidity, the relations began to develop on an even keel. Visits were exchanged,[1] international affairs were amiably discussed, and a number of agreements were signed, the most important of which was the agreement on Tibet (April 1954) that contained the five principles of peaceful coexistence.[2]

It would of course be presumptuous to attribute the change in China's policy exclusively to Indian patience and initiative. Obviously, there was a host of different factors and circumstances that must have contributed to the formulation of the new policy. None the less, the Indian factor is important in so far as it was India's determination to adopt an independent line on many controversial issues concerning China that led her decision-makers to appreciate the importance of non-alignment in international affairs.

Undoubtedly, this important change in the Chinese attitude towards India and her policy of non-alignment was the first major breakthrough for Indian diplomacy; for it disintegrated the monolithic view which was hitherto rampant among the Communist countries, and inaugurated a new policy towards the non-Communist countries of Asia.

[1] Chou En-lai visited India in June 1954 and Nehru returned the visit in October of the same year.

[2] Government of India, *op. cit.*, pp. 85–93.

CHAPTER III

PEACEFUL COEXISTENCE
Political Relations

(a) *Change in Moscow's Attitude*

Within a year after the shift in China's policy, the Soviet Union also began to show signs of moderating her attitude towards the non-Communist nations of Asia. Evidently, it was hardly expedient for the Moscow leaders to continue the old and rather unsuccessful line, when China, the largest and the most powerful Communist nation in Asia, had decided to blaze a new and benign path. For one thing, it would have only further aggravated Soviet isolation from Asia, leaving the field wide open for China to increase her influence in the area. For another, it would have generated serious differences among the Asian Communists who were already showing some signs of bemusement after the inauguration of the rather uncoordinated process of de-Stalinization in the Soviet Union.

Perhaps the most decisive reason that led to an innovation in Soviet policy, however, was the disastrous consequences that had resulted from the pursuit of the militant line. Almost all the Asian Communist parties, who had thoughtlessly followed the Soviet call for revolution in 1948–49, were isolated from the mainstream of Asian policies. In Indonesia, the Communist party ceased to have any influence in the aftermath of the abortive Madiun revolt of September 1948. In Burma, it was stagnating, deeply riven with factional conflicts. In Malaya, it was facing serious difficulties and reduced from a peak of about 8,000 to a few hundred stragglers. In the Philippines, after a brief period of popularity and strength, it was on the run with military power completely broken. And in India, where it had, over the years, established impressive footholds among the workers, peasants and intellectuals, the feckless revolts, organized under the leadership of B. T. Ranadive and later Rajeswar Rao—one centering around the workers and the other around the peasants—plummeted its prestige to an all-time low, sharply declining its membership from an estimated 89,263 to 20,000.[1]

It is evident that the attraction and influence of nationalism was too strong and too deeply rooted among the Asian people to be overthrown by artificially created revolutionary upheavals. And the Communist parties, though sufficiently powerful to create confusion in their respective countries, were not strong enough to take over the reins of power. Even where they had become viable factors, and had successfully acquired a dominant position, it was because they had fervently advocated national-istic objectives. The Chinese Communists had successfully seized power not so much because of their attractive economic and social objectives, but because of the effective manner in which they tried to meet the national aspirations of the Chinese people during the entire period of Japanese aggression. And Ho chi-minh's successful defiance of France was primarily due to the projection of a nationalist image rather than to his Communist proclivities. 'The strength of Communism wherever it is in practice', aptly pointed out Nehru, 'is partly due to its association with the national spirit. Where the two are dissociated, Communism is relatively weak except in so far as it embodies the discontent that exists in under-developed and poverty-stricken countries.'[2]

The setback encountered by Asian Communists generally was, how-ever, not only due to their failure to project an acceptable nationalist image. It was also because of their inability to comprehend the social content of nationalist movements. Many of the Asian leaders, having been impressed at some stage of their political lives by the October revolution, had openly and firmly proclaimed their intention to introduce a much more far-reaching socialist pattern of society in their countries than had been intended by the socialist leaders of the West. Evidently, the framework of Asian socialism—both of the left and right variety—was different from the European movements in so far as the Asians stressed their basic cultural values, generally pursued a policy of non-alignment, and operated in developing societies of teeming millions and low technology. On social and economic problems though seeking some goals, they showed greater determination to re-structure their tradition-bound societies than the European socialists. Clearly, this was in many ways a significant development which merited rational analysis. But the contemptuous and rather hasty identification of it with capitalism not only had demonstrated the extent of Soviet dogmatism, but had also

---

[1] Overstreet and Windmiller, *Communism in India* (Berkeley: 1959), p. 357.

[2] Jawaharlal Nehru, *India Today and Tomorrow* (New Delhi: 1960), p. 17.

exposed a lack of political sophistication that is vital for the understanding of new trends, new thoughts and new movements. All these factors thus did not leave much choice for the Soviet leaders. They had to introduce some policy changes and project a new image of themselves if they wished to exercise any effective influence in areas which were not under their direct control.

Already during the last few months of the Stalinist epoch, subtle signs had become evident that the Soviet leadership was prepared to relax tension on the international scene. Stalin was personally prepared to meet with President-elect Eisenhower in December 1952, and the Nineteenth Congress of the Communist Party of the Soviet Union held in October 1952, though still critical of the West, appeared to generate a general atmosphere of moderation. Towards Asia, too, a decided change had become apparent. The Soviet Government increasingly underlined the importance of inter-state relations and appeared favourably to view some of the diplomatic actions of the Asian governments.[1]

As far as India was concerned, the new thinking initially manifested itself in relatively minor matters. For instance, the Soviet Government, which had so far kept aloof, suddenly agreed, at the beginning of 1952, to build a Russian pavilion at the International Industries Fair in Bombay, and expressed willingness to make capital goods available to India.[2] Indian businessmen were invited to attend the International Economic Conference, held in April 1952 in Moscow,[3] and a shipment of wheat, rice and condensed milk was sent by the Soviet trade unions.[4] Stalin, who had not met any foreign diplomat for almost two years, granted a parting interview to the Indian Ambassador, Dr Radhakrishnan, on 5 April of the same year;[5] and the Soviet Government promptly gave its accord to the appointment of K. P. S. Menon as the new Indian Ambassador in Moscow.[6]

The occurrence of such minor events in a non-Communist society may not be considered of any particular importance, but they are significant in the case of the Soviet Union, where important changes are often preceded by a series of minor innovations.

It was, however, the death of Stalin which heralded striking innovations

[1] For some details see Charles McLane, *Soviet Strategies in South-East Asia* (New Jersey: 1966), pp. 455–73.

[2] *India Record* (28 February 1952).   [3] *Ibid.*

[4] K. P. Karunakaran, *India in World Affairs 1950–53* (Calcutta: 1958), p. 239.

[5] *India Record* (28 February 1952).

[6] K. P. S. Menon, *The Flying Troika* (London: 1963), p. 2.

in Soviet policy. More and more flexibility, imagination and vigour became apparent. Internally the oppressive and harsh aspects of Stalinist legacy were quickly set aside; and externally a series of concrete diplomatic steps was taken to relax the suffocating tension that dominated the world political scene.

So far as India was concerned the first important and formal sign of Soviet change was manifested in August 1953, when Malenkov, in his speech to the Supreme Soviet, praised India's role in the Korean armistice agreement. He declared:

The stand taken by such a big country as India is of great significance for the consolidation of peace in the East. India had made her own significant contribution to the efforts of the peace-loving countries directed to the ending of war in Korea. Our relations with India are growing stronger, and cultural and economic ties are developing. India and the Soviet Union will continue to develop and strengthen, with friendly co-operation as their key note.[1]

The contrast in this speech between severe criticism of the United States and a friendly reference to the new states of Asia gave a hint that the new Soviet leaders recognized the potential value of a friendly approach to the national governments of Asia.

The new government in Moscow lost no time in giving a concrete shift to its policy. In the summer of 1953, an Indian art exhibition was held in Moscow at the request of the Soviet Government.[2] In October 1953, the new Soviet Ambassador to New Delhi, M. A. Menshikov, handed a cheque of about 60,000 dollars to Nehru for the national relief fund,[3] and placed a wreath on the tomb of Gandhi, an important gesture which his predecessor, Novikov, had carefully avoided.[4] In the same month, he offered to supply India with industrial equipment, farm machinery and tools at prices more favourable than those prevailing in the West. In exchange for these commodities, Menshikov, on behalf of his government, agreed to buy jute and tea, for which there was at that time a great slack in the West because of the Korean armistice. On 2 December, an important trade agreement was signed with India. It was intended to be in force for five years, and bound the two governments to

---

[1] *Pravda* (9 August 1953).   [2] K. P. S. Menon, *op. cit.*, pp. 17, 63.

[3] *New Times* (31 October 1953), p. 32.

[4] G. Mittel, 'The Second Cultural Offensive in India', *Studies in the Soviet Union* (July 1957), p. 119.

facilitate trade between the two countries over a wide range of goods. The important characteristic of this agreement, however, was the Soviet acceptance to allow the Indians to pay in rupees for the goods imported from the USSR.[1]

Mutual visits were also encouraged. India's Health Minister, Raj Kumari Amrit Kaur, was invited to visit Moscow. The visit was significant in so far as it was the first time that a Minister in the Central Government was officially invited by the Soviet authorities. On her return to India, she publicly stated that the Soviet Union wished to have 'warm friendly relations with India'.[2] In the following month, Nehru's daughter, Indira Gandhi, visited the Soviet Union. She travelled extensively in the country for almost two months, and was the first foreigner permitted to visit the Central Asian Republics. After her return, she also testified to the existence of warm feelings towards India.[3] By the end of 1954 as many as fourteen Indian delegations, from a football team and film artists to industrialists, had already visited Moscow at the invitation of the Soviet Government.

(b) *India turns to Moscow*

All these developments undoubtedly generated an atmosphere of friendliness, increasing the number and variety of contacts between the two nations. But these contacts and relations were none the less limited to economic and cultural spheres. Viable and meaningful political links were still non-existent; and the factors and circumstances that normally provide the necessary impetus for bringing nations closer politically were still missing. But this did not last long; for a number of new factors surged up on the international scene which opened the door for the forging of close political ties between the two countries. Interestingly enough this was provided by the United States in 1954. During that year, Washington, in an effort to negate some of the inherent weaknesses apparent in South-east Asia and the Middle East, devoted a considerable part of its efforts to the building of military alliances. The South-east Asia Collective Defence Treaty was signed on 8 September 1954 by the United States, Great Britain, France, Australia, New Zealand, the Philippines, Thailand and Pakistan; and under active encouragement from Washington, elements of a 'northern tier' defence system, embracing

---

[1] For complete text see *Foreign Affairs Reports* (December 1959).
[2] *Pravda* (22 June 1953).   [3] *Ibid.* (30 August 1953).

Turkey, Pakistan, Iran and Iraq also emerged in 1954. Furthermore, significant military assistance was furnished to Pakistan.

To New Delhi, the notion of a defence alliance to protect South-east Asia and the Middle East against a possible Chinese or Soviet attack was abhorrent on many counts. First such an alliance contradicted India's passionately held view that military blocs generally were a step towards war rather than peace. Secondly, the projected inclusion of Pakistan threatened to introduce a system of military blocs into India's immediate neighbourhood, thus converting the sub-continent into a theatre of cold war at the very time when New Delhi was making strenuous efforts to make it the centre of an Asian 'peace area'. Thirdly, the prospect of United States military assistance to Pakistan threatened to strengthen that country not only in relation to the Soviet Union with whom she had no quarrel, but in relation to India with whom important and explosive issues were still outstanding.

Therefore, despite all assurances from the United States that military assistance to Pakistan was not and would not be directed against India, Nehru lost no opportunity to reaffirm his wholehearted distaste for the project.[1] On 3 January 1955, he expressed great concern and warned the West that military assistance to Pakistan might affect many balances already existing in the area.[2] On 9 February, he characterized American diplomacy in the area 'as the return of Western powers to the Asian front'.[3]

Inevitably, all these developments germinated some changes in India's policy towards the outside world. First, a wave of anti-American sentiment swept the country, alienating many segments of Indian public opinion which had been sympathetic to the United States. In fact, so intense was this feeling of anti-Americanism that even the relatively moderate Nehru government was affected by it—so much so that the United Nations was advised to remove its officers of American nationality stationed in Kashmir, since they were no longer considered as neutral in the Kashmir dispute.[4]

Secondly, India began to devote a considerable part of her diplomatic efforts to bring together all like-minded countries with the object of giving definite shape to non-alignment as an international force. There

[1] The Government of India was informed by the United States Government on 17 November 1953 that it was considering a military agreement with Pakistan. India was thus informed six months before the conclusion of the agreement. For details see G. W. Choudhury, *Pakistan's Relations with India 1947–66* (London: 1969), p. 233.

[2] *India News* (9 January 1954).   [3] *Ibid.* (13 February 1954).   [4] *Ibid.* (20 March 1954).

does not seem to be any doubt that the United States' activities in the area threw into relief, and each other's company, those nations which for one reason or another found it more convenient to occupy the no-man's land between the western and the Communist blocs than to attach themselves to either. The Brioni conference held in July 1956 between Nehru, Nasser and Tito, for example, was the striking example of the concert that began to develop between the three principal partisans of non-alignment. It was this conference that encouraged them to rally all the non-aligned forces for the purposes of projecting a joint approach on numerous issues of international affairs.

Thirdly, India began to show definite signs of moving closer to China and Moscow, the most important indications of which were Nehru's visit to Peking in 1954 and his acceptance of the Soviet invitation to visit the Soviet Union.

(c) *Soviet diplomatic offensive*

Moscow, equally opposed to American efforts to build anti-Communist alliances, naturally viewed Indian opposition as an excellent opportunity to further cultivate with India, and exploit the rising anti-American feeling that was manifesting in the country. Nehru's severe criticism of the United States military aid to Pakistan did not go unnoticed. On the contrary, wide coverage was given to his views in the Soviet press. A *Pravda* article wrote:

The Indian people cannot but be alarmed seeing the attempts to set up an aggressive bloc right on India's borders, which will invariably lead to the building of foreign bases and airfields on the territories of India's neighbours and to the militarization of these countries with which it is attempting to maintain close relations.[1]

A massive Soviet offensive for friendship with India was thus launched; and Soviet writers who, only a few years earlier, had made it a point to stress the unfortunate aspects of Indian life, began to emphasize the positive features of India. Suddenly, they found that 'everything in India attracts the artist's eye'.[2] Those who had in the past written about India's slums and filthy streets now mentioned 'the fine buildings which to this day are like a hymn of man's genius'.[3] In an effort to create a proper

[1] *Pravda* (27 September 1953).   [2] *New Times* (7 August 1954), pp. 27–9.   [3] *Ibid.*

atmosphere between the two countries, Soviet historians began to underline the great importance that was attached by Lenin to the revolutionary
movement in India.[1] They also suddenly discovered that Afanasi Nikitin,
a subject of the Tsar, had visited India in 1469–72. Since it was appropriate
and timely to give him credit for this adventure, he was duly made a
national hero. In the presence of the Indian Ambassador, a statue of
Nikitin was unveiled in Kalinan in May 1955.[2] Mahatma Gandhi, who
had so far been consistently condemned as reactionary in Soviet publications, was now praised for his progressive and important role in the
national struggle. 'We know', said Bulganin in a speech to the Indian
Parliament in November 1955, 'how greatly important in that struggle
were the ideas and the guidance of the distinguished leader of the Indian
national movement, Mahatma Gandhi.'[3] At the twentieth party congress
of the Communist Party of the Soviet Union, Kuusinnen had gone even
further and proposed a serious reassessment of Gandhi's role in the Indian
nationalist movement.[4]

It was perhaps in the diplomatic field that the change in Soviet policy
was most striking. No longer was India's foreign policy considered to be
tied to the apron strings of the West, and no longer was Nehru considered
a reactionary serving the interests of the imperialists. On the contrary,
Soviet official declarations and articles in the press were now full of
praise for India and her approach to world problems. Hardly an occasion
was missed to underline her important role in international affairs. During
Nehru's visit to the Soviet Union in June 1955, the Soviet public was
mobilized to give him a reception 'for which there has been no parallel
in Moscow before or since'.[5]

As a part of this diplomatic offensive, the Soviet Government extended
complete support to India on the two foreign policy issues—Kashmir and
Goa—that faced her in the mid-fifties. Unlike the West, whose attitude
on these issues was, to say the least, ambivalent, the Soviet Government
came out openly and categorically on the side of India. This became
evident during Khruschev's and Bulganin's visit to India in 1955. For
Khruschev, the Kashmir problem had already been resolved by the people
of the area,[6] and it was only a question of time before 'Goa will free

---

[1] *Pravda* (21 April 1954).   [2] K. P. S. Menon, *op. cit.*, pp. 17, 117.
[3] N. A. Bulganin and N. S. Khruschev, *Speeches during sojourn in India, Burma and Afghanistan* (New Delhi: 1956).
[4] *Stenograficheski Otchet XX ovo Kongressa KRSS* (Moscow: 1957), Vol. I, p. 503.
[5] K. P. S. Menon, *op. cit.*, p. 106.
[6] See N. A. Bulganin and N. S. Khruschev, *op. cit.*, p. 73.

D

itself from foreign rule and will become an integral part of the Republic of India'.[1]

At the Security Council of the United Nations too, the Soviet delegation extended full support to India. When the representatives of the United States, the United Kingdom, Australia, Colombia and Cuba tabled a resolution reiterating their wish to hold plebiscite under United Nations auspices, the Soviet representative stated unambiguously that the Kashmiri people considered themselves 'to be an inalienable part of the Republic of India'.[2] The Soviet delegate, however, did not veto the Anglo-American resolution, as it was only an attempt to reiterate the Council's earlier position. But when the same group of countries tabled another resolution suggesting that the use of United Nations force to implement the plebiscite deserved serious consideration, the Soviet Government did not hesitate to block the resolution.[3] Again in 1962, when an attempt was made to reintroduce the Kashmir issue in the Security Council on the grounds that India had plans to capture that part of Kashmir that was under Pakistani control, the Soviet representative opposed the proposal and promptly vetoed the Irish resolution which proposed a plebiscite.[4]

On the Goa issue too, Soviet Russia extended complete support to India. When the Indian troops occupied Goa, Diu, Daman, Khruschev promptly sent a message to New Delhi expressing his government's complete support of the Indian action;[5] and when the Security Council, with western support, took up the Goa issue to censure India, the Soviet delegation once again promptly used its power to veto the resolution.[6]

The Soviet support on Kashmir and Goa was undoubtedly a very significant development; for it not only strengthened the Indian determination to maintain its position on these issues, but made it possible to resist effectively the political pressures that continuously emanated from the West, demanding concessions on these issues.

However, in addition to these distinct advantages, the task of Indian diplomacy was generally made easier. The wooing of India by the two Communist giants not only made it possible for her to disengage partially

---

[1] See N. A. Bulganin and N. S. Khruschev, *op. cit.*, p. 73.

[2] *Official Records of the Security Council of the United Nations January–March 1957*, Document S/3779 (New York: 1958).

[3] *Ibid.*, Document S/3787.

[4] *Ibid.*, Document S/5134.

[5] *Pravda* (22 December 1961).   [6] *Ibid.* (27 January 1962).

from an excessive dependence on the West, but generated the necessary climate for an effective implementation of the policy of non-alignment. Having now been accepted by both the blocs—though the West perhaps had some reservations—it was now possible for India to project herself on the international scene, to play a greater role in decreasing tension, to propose solutions that would not be rejected outright, and to bring conflicting parties together to resolve their differences. Towards the end of the Korean War, for example, she was able to defreeze the tense atmosphere between the belligerents. At the 1954 Geneva conference the Indian delegation was able to generate the proper atmosphere which finally led to the conclusion of agreements on the three states that constitute Indo-China. And at the Bogor conference of Asian Prime Ministers, Nehru was successful in obtaining an invitation for China to participate at the Afro-Asian conference that was held in Bandung in 1955.

It is therefore not surprising that the change in Soviet policy was considered a major landmark in world politics since 1945, and did not fail to generate a climate of friendliness in both countries. During Nehru's visit to the Soviet Union in 1955, the Soviet Government did not leave any stone unturned to dramatize his presence in the Soviet Union. Many a foreign statesman has travelled to Moscow since the revolution. For them, there were the usual official receptions, but the man in the street knew little about their visits until they read about them in the newspapers. The reception given to Nehru was unprecedented. When he arrived in Moscow in the afternoon of 7 June 1955, the entire Presidium turned up at the airport to receive him. All Moscow, it seemed, had also turned out. In all factories to which he went, workers in their thousands gathered to have a glimpse of him. At one place, according to an eye witness, 'the crowd was so huge that he was unable to enter a factory and returned to it three hours later, after the people had dispersed'.[1] In fact the measure of Soviet receptivity to Nehru's visit was so great that they proposed that the joint Indo-Soviet statement should be entirely drafted by the Indian delegation.[2]

When Khruschev and Bulganin visited India in November and December of the same year, unprecedented welcome was also given to them. At the biggest function in Delhi, more than 500,000 people turned up and at Calcutta more than three million people over-flowed the city, setting all police arrangements to naught.

[1] K. P. S. Menon, 'Steady Growth of Relations', in V. V. Balubuschevich and Bimla Prasad, *India and the Soviet Union. A Symposium* (New Delhi: 1969), p. 26.
[2] *Ibid.*, p. 27.

All these public manifestations of friendship emanating from both sides considerably contributed to the breaking up of the unfriendly barriers that had separated the two countries only a few years earlier. In fact, according to an opinion poll, conducted in three areas shortly after the visit of Khruschev and Bulganin, there was a considerable change in Indian attitude towards Moscow. Sixty-two per cent of the public in Calcutta, 42·03 per cent in Travancore and 22·05 per cent in Delhi had altered their views on the Soviet Union.[1]

Having successfully developed the bonds of friendship with India, the Soviet leaders strove to project her increasingly on the international scene, presumably in the hope of obtaining her support on many controversial issues on which they had strong views. In the first place, they openly began to strive for the increasing association of India in talks with big powers on disarmament and on Asian issues. At the Geneva conference of 1954, they favoured the formal participation of India.[2] But this was prevented by the United States who did not appear to have any confidence in India's objectivity—least of all in Krishna Menon who was unofficially present in Geneva during the conference. In November 1956, Moscow proposed the convening of a summit conference on disarmament in which, apart from the big four, India would be present.[3] In a covering letter to the Prime Minister of India, Bulganin stated that he highly valued 'the role played by India and Nehru himself in strengthening world peace' and expressed the hope that the note would receive India's due consideration. During the Middle Eastern crisis of 1958, Khruschev sent messages to the United States of America, the United Kingdom, France and India, proposing that the 'heads of governments of USSR, US, UK, France and India should meet without delay . . . in order to take measures to end the present military conflict'.[4] In a separate letter to Nehru, Khruschev made a pointed reference to India's role in world affairs:

We in the Soviet Union know India as one of the leading states, a country whose voice is heeded not only in Asia, but throughout the world. The Soviet government hopes that you will do everything possible to facilitate successive collective efforts by the peace-loving states to avert the catastrophe while it can still be averted. By supporting the proposal for an

[1] *Monthly Public Opinion Survey*, Nos. 7, 8, 9 (1956).
[2] T. S. George, *Khrisna Menon. A Biography* (Bombay: 1966), p. 210.
[3] *New Times*, No. 48 (1958), Supplement.
[4] *New Times*, No. 30 (1958), Supplement.

immediate conference and by her active participation in it, India will make an inestimable contribution to the preservation of peace.[1]

Soviet diplomacy also strove to introduce an element of co-ordination between Indian and Soviet policies in the whole gamut of international affairs. At the Geneva conference on Vietnam, efforts were made to seek common understanding, and at the London conference on Suez a broad measure of co-operation increasingly became apparent.

That India had gained considerable diplomatic advantage from the forging of closer ties with the Soviet Union is evident. But there were none the less a certain number of disadvantages that usually result from the development of too close a relationship with another country. In order to safeguard these relations, nations often become less critical and less objective in their assessment of the policy of other friendly nations. India, for example, avoided any criticism of the Soviet Union on actions that she adopted on issues that concerned her directly. The advantages accruing to India from Soviet projection of India on the international scene, and Soviet support on Kashmir and Goa obviously outweighed the disadvantages that would have resulted from an Indian criticism of the Soviet Union.

Consider the Indian attitude towards the Soviet invasion of Hungary. The Indian delegation to the United Nations, led by Menon, declined to support the different resolutions proposed in the General Assembly which were critical of Soviet intervention in Hungary, and which proposed the holding of elections under the auspices of the United Nations. Nehru himself was careful in expressing views on the Hungarian situation. While mildly criticizing some of the Soviet actions, he cleverly neutralized any adverse effect such an expression might have had on the Soviet Union by referring to the instigations that emanated from the outside—including the smuggling of arms.[2] Undoubtedly, the holding of free elections in Hungary, under United Nations supervision, would have created a dangerous precedent so far as the future of Kashmir was concerned, but it was certainly not the only reason that influenced Indian policy on the Hungarian crisis. The fear of a general adverse Soviet reaction was in all probability another important factor that determined India's benign attitude.

Again when the Soviets resumed the suspended nuclear tests, Nehru,

[1] New Times, No. 30 (1958), Supplement.
[2] Jawaharlal Nehru, Jawaharlal Nehru Speeches, Vol. III, March 1953–August 1957 (New Delhi: 1958), pp. 321–340.

who was visiting the Soviet Union, after having attended the non-aligned conference in Belgrade, was careful in his criticism of the Soviet Union, and expressed his views in very general terms, stating that the neutral leaders who had delegated him were 'distressed and deeply concerned at the deterioration in the international situation'.[1]

However, it was not so much on concrete issues that the Indian Government avoided criticizing Moscow, for there were indeed very few international problems on which there was any serious disagreement between the two governments. It was the general Indian prudence towards Moscow that was more striking and that appeared to encourage many in the West to charge India of following double standards. Very rarely during the period was the Soviet Union criticized by the Indian decision-makers. Hardly ever was any effort made to underline some of the basic issues that separated New Delhi from Moscow. And at no point was the Soviet Union ever charged with pursuing an unacceptable political line.

Obviously, the advantages to India of Indo–Soviet friendship were too great and too vital to be abandoned by fruitlessly taking issue with Moscow on problems that really did not concern Indian interests. The Soviet leaders, unused to criticism from their friends and accustomed to functioning in a close society, would have reacted strongly to criticism on issues that did not concern the Indian Government.

[1] *Pravda* (9 September 1961).

CHAPTER IV

PEACEFUL COEXISTENCE

Economic Relations

The Soviet diplomatic actions in support of India, though undoubtedly effective for generating a favourable image, were apparently not sufficient to orient India in the direction of Moscow. For she was indeed inhibited in her goal of achieving real and effective disengagement from the West due to her excessive economic dependence on Great Britain and the United States. Practically all her aid until the mid-fifties came from the West, and almost all her trade was geared to western markets. Admittedly, the Indian leaders were aware of the considerable difficulties that such a situation created in the implementation of a viable independent foreign policy, but they could hardly remedy this situation in view of the apparent Soviet aversion to non-aligned India in the late forties and early fifties. Thus, notwithstanding the official declarations proclaiming India's determination to pursue an independent policy, her options in real terms were still severely circumscribed. Hardly could she consider disengaging herself from the West in the absence of any meaningful alternatives.

However, after the death of Stalin and with the rapid inauguration of an over-all moderate policy, the forging of economic links with India and other non-aligned countries became the key lever of Soviet foreign policy. An ideological justification for the new policy was soon found by the introduction of some important innovations in the Soviet approach to the problems of development.

During the Stalinist approach, the Soviet leaders did not consider that the decolonization process that had commenced in the aftermath of World War II had brought real independence to India, in view of her economic dependence on the West. The transfer of power was characterized as a compromise among the British imperialists, the big Indian bourgeoisie and the landlords.[1] Through such an arrangement, argued the Soviet ideologists, the British monopoly capitalists tried to safeguard

[1] E. Varga, *Osnovnye voprosy ekonomikii i politiki imperializma posle vtoroj mirovoy voiny* (Moscow: 1953), pp. 330–31.

their economic position with the assistance of the Indian governing classes; and the latter defended their interests in co-operation with the imperialists against the workers and peasant movements.[1]

Real political independence was therefore not possible as long as India was economically dependent, and this in the Soviet view was unlikely under the existing national leadership which was too closely tied with the West. The only way to achieve real independence was through 'a struggle of all the working people with the proletariat in the vanguard led by the Communist Party'.[2]

After the death of Stalin, this assessment, however, underwent a significant change. Though India was still considered dependent on the West,[3] and was criticized for facilitating the influx of foreign capital,[4] her economy was however no longer considered to be dominated by foreign monopoly capital and the big bourgeoisie. In its place, there had developed, in the Soviet view, the new phenomenon of state capitalism which 'has a definite progressive significance' in so far as it helps to accelerate India's economic development,[5] shortens the period of primitive accumulation of capital[6] and weakens the position of foreign capital in the country.[7]

Obviously, in the Soviet view, the process of economic development should be encouraged by the working class—though still continuing to struggle against the bourgeoisie—by extending support to certain measures of the bourgeois state,[8] and by forging economic links with the socialist countries in order 'to strengthen democratic anti-imperialist features of the State sector, leading to a certain degree of independence from the imperialists and the local reactionaries who exhibit monopolist tendencies'.[9]

The new evaluation of the Indian economic and social structure was thus brought in line with the new and moderate policy implemented by Stalin's successors. And a reliance on the more subtle instruments of

---

[1] E. Varga, op. cit.

[2] Ibid., p. 362.

[3] For details see V. I. Pavlov, India: Economic Freedom versus Imperialism (New Delhi: 1963).

[4] See Sofia Melman, Foreign Monopoly Capital in Indian Economy (New Delhi: 1963).

[5] Pavlov, op. cit., p. 32.

[6] Nezavisimaja Indija 10 let nezavisimosti 1947–1957 sbornik statej (Moscow: 1958), p. 32.

[7] Ibid.

[8] For a detailed analysis of the question, see Stephen Clarkson, L'analyse sovietique des problèmes indiens du sous-développement (Paris: 1965), Ph.D. dissertation.

[9] Pavlov, op. cit., p. 44.

economic and political diplomacy was considered more effective and more appropriate to the new situation.

An unprecedented Soviet offensive was therefore launched with the specific purpose of forging economic links. Trade was sedulously developed and important economic assistance was given.

(a) Soviet trade

The net result of this offensive was the remarkable rise in trade turnover between the two countries. From a negligible figure of 8·1 million rupees in 1953, it increased to 719·7 million rupees in 1961, to 1753·6 million in 1965,[1] to 2269·5 million in 1966–67,[2] and to 4970 million rupees at the end of 1968.[3] According to the commercial agreement for 1966–67, signed on 7 January 1966, the trade between the two countries was expected to double by 1970 as compared to 1964.[4] Considering the general expansion that is expected in the Soviet trade turnover by 1980, it has been suggested by some specialists that India could in fact 'hopefully increase her turnover of trade to more than double, if she can harness and develop capacity to produce various items needed in the Soviet Union'.[5]

It is evident that there was a favourable constellation of factors that contributed to this rapid rise: there was the Soviet determination to develop relations and there was also the fact that the rapid rate of growth was accounted by the low level from which it had started fifteen years earlier. None the less, the rate of growth is too significant to be attributable only to the absence of any relations in 1953 or to such elements as political determination. There were obviously a number of concrete economic reasons that contributed to the rapid rise of trade between the two countries.

In the first place, the Russians not only accepted India's traditional exports but also her newly produced items. This includes footwear, household goods, sewing machines, fans, electric appliances, oil engines, rolled ferrous stock, razor blades, air conditioners, etc.[6] The list of

[1] Yearbook of International Trade Statistics (New York: 1967), p. 391.
[2] The Statesman's Year Book, 1968–1969 (New York: 1968), p. 381.
[3] B. R. Bhagat, 'Indo-Soviet Trade. Promising prospects ahead', Commerce (11 April 1970).
[4] Soviet News (11 January 1966).
[5] Ministry of Commerce, India's Trade with East Europe (New Delhi: 1966), p. 45.
[6] Economic Times (16 May 1964).

commodities finalized in the January 1966 protocol also provided for the export of some other manufactures such as electric lamps, engineering products, machine tools, textiles, etc.[1]

The increasing share of manufactured and semi-manufactured goods in Soviet imports from India had undoubtedly become a significant feature of Indo-Soviet trade. If in 1956 they accounted for 18 per cent of India's exports to the USSR, in 1963 this increased to 30 per cent and in 1966 almost reached 45 per cent.[2] The trend is expected to continue. Under the commercial agreement for 1966–70, signed in January 1966, nearly half of India's exports are expected to consist of finished and semi-finished goods by 1970.[3]

Secondly, since 1959, all transactions, commercial and non-commercial, with Moscow are settled in non-convertible Indian rupees. The rupee payments for Soviet exports are entered in Soviet accounts in Indian banks and then are used for Indian exports to the USSR. It is difficult to overestimate the importance of this system of payment in view of the fact that for a nation like India, which is suffering from a huge deficit of hard foreign currency, it has considerably helped in the scaling down of the continuous deficit that she has with the Soviet Union.

One cannot escape the reflection that the remarkably rapid quantitative and qualitative increase in the trade turnover between the two countries has greatly contributed to the effective implementation of the Indian policy of non-alignment; for India is no longer exclusively dependent on the West. Furthermore, it has opened important channels for obtaining machinery and technical know-how without having to spend convertible currency. That this is an important development is evident from the fact that the continuous paucity of convertible currency had in the past created serious bottlenecks in her development plans.

The opening up of the vast socialist market has also made it possible for India to market many products which the western markets cannot absorb. For a nation which is on the verge of economic take-off, this is a very important development.

It has been argued that an increase of trade with the socialist countries has resulted in a diversion of trade from the market economy countries, leading to restriction on the acquisition of convertible foreign exchange. Such an argument, however, does not hold water, for commodity-by-

[1] For complete text see Ministry of Commerce, *India's Trade Agreements with Other Countries* (New Delhi: 1968), pp. 340–1.

[2] V. I. Smirnov, 'A New Era in World History', *Indian Express* (7 November 1968).

[3] *Soviet News* (10 January 1968), p. 23.

commodity investigation of some of the principal exportable items (tobacco, jute, tea, coffee) has shown the difficulties of marketing more than what had already been done in the market economy areas.[1] In any case, the Indian export incentive scheme is framed in such a way that the exporters to the convertible currency areas get more encouragement than exporters to socialist countries. In other words, they are operating under bigger inducements to export to these areas. If they still export to the socialist countries, they do so to overcome their inability to sell their goods in the convertible currency areas.

Bilateralism, however, has one major defect. For the sole purpose of achieving a balance of trade and payments, a country might sometimes be compelled to make unsuitable purchases from her bilateral trade partner.[2] India has already begun to face this difficulty. Currently she is running a surplus of rupees (250 million) with the Soviet Union, and with the prospective upsurge in the export of railway wagons[3] and engineering items the trade balance is likely to turn even more favourable. The Indian economy, having become more sophisticated, is in the need of importing more and more raw materials which the Soviet Union is not in a position to supply. Following the principle of balancing her trade and payments, India thus may be compelled to make unsuitable purchases, thus failing to make maximum use of export earnings.

Some of the socialist countries have already become aware of this difficulty. In fact, Poland, Hungary, Bulgaria and Rumania have already accepted the principle of triangular settlements.[4] And considering the fact that this principle has already been accepted by the Soviet Union in the case of Brazil,[5] she might do the same in the case of India too.

The introduction of an element of multilateralism into rupee trade opens up possibilities of evolving a payment system for rupee trade with rupees as the currency, somewhat on the pattern of the arrangements governing trade with the sterling area. In the course of time, the rupee could be used to balance trade even between third countries in which India is not a party. Such multilateralism of trade and payments will increase the

[1] For details see *India's trade, op. cit.*

[2] For a study of this problem see Carole A. Sawyer, *Communist Trade with Developing Countries 1955–1965* (New York: 1967), pp. 67–8.

[3] The Soviet Government is negotiating an agreement with the Indian Government to buy large quantities of railway wagons.

[4] *Economic and Political Weekly* (9 November 1968).

[5] Sawyer, *op. cit.*, p. 63.

efficiency of trade within the rupee payment bloc by making it possible to import from the cheapest source and to export at the highest price without having to aim at balanced trade with every single partner.

(b) Soviet aid

In the case of aid, too, the Soviet contribution to Indian economic development is undoubtedly significant. By 1967, Soviet credits totalled well over 10 billion rupees and made India the recipient of by far the largest amount of Soviet foreign aid (exclusive of arms). Admittedly, the total assistance emanating from Moscow is less than the aid given by Washington; but its impact on Indian economy is undoubtedly greater. By and large, most Indians tend to agree with the view that the aid coming from Moscow was more favourable and more approximate to Indian economic needs and thinking.

Although such a widely held view may be partly attributable to the remarkably well-organized publicity campaign concerning Soviet economic assistance, it is none the less principally due to the considerable advantage that actually accrues from such aid.

In the first place, Soviet economic assistance is primarily concentrated on heavy industry in the public sector—an area to which the Indian decision-makers, rightly or wrongly, have given top priority. In fact, most of the expansion of Indian heavy industry has been due to the direct or indirect assistance emanating from Moscow. Even a cursory glance at the Indian economic plans would show that Soviet assistance is concentrated on the building up of steel plants, on the exploring and refining of oil, and on the development of heavy engineering and electrical equipment plants. Furthermore, Soviet assistance is geared to the objective of establishing industrial complexes rather than individual plants. This has involved assistance for the development of ancillary industries not only horizontally but also vertically. For example, in connexion with the construction of steel plant, provision has been made for the development of raw material resources, the creation of power supply, the production of coal needed for the metallurgical and power industries, and the setting up even of heavy machine building plants. All this has gone a long way in laying the foundation of a self-reliant industrial growth, and in the building of the infrastructure to encourage and sustain the development of industries in other sectors.

Secondly, most of the credits given by Russia to India—the interest on which does not exceed 2·5 per cent—were long-term credits,[1] the repayment of which would begin one year after the completion of deliveries of the equipment.[2] Such an arrangement makes it possible for India to incorporate Soviet assistance in her planning and establish her plans for a number of years. Moreover, the repayment of Soviet credits is either in Indian rupees or in goods. In certain cases, it has also been possible to make repayments by exporting goods produced in plants set up by Soviet assistance.[3] For a country like India which has a considerable debt in foreign currency, such an arrangement for repayment is of particular significance, as it opens the possibility of developing her foreign trade.

Thirdly, economic co-operation agreements with the Soviet Union have been in most cases package deals involving assistance for the projection and elaboration of blueprints for the plants concerned, for the supply of raw material components and machinery, and for the supply of technical documentation, including know-how. The implementation of these package deals has meant the transfer of technology on a gigantic scale, by the close association of Indian engineers and technicians with the designing, construction and operation of the plants, and by the training of more than 2,000 Indians in Soviet universities and plants.

The general advantages of Soviet aid were thus considerable, and it would therefore be useful at this stage perhaps to see a little more closely the type of Soviet assistance that is given to build some of the basic industries.

STEEL

Soviet aid to India began with a flourish. On 2 February 1955, Moscow agreed to build a steel mill at Bhilai with an annual capacity of one million tons.[4] The conclusion of such an agreement placed India in a better position to negotiate with western firms, for as long as the Soviet

---

[1] For details see V. Rymalov, *La collaboration économique de l'URSS avec les pays sous-développés* (Moscow: n.d.).

[2] For details see Indian Ministry of Finance, *Text of agreement between the government of India and the government of the USSR, signed on 21 February 1961, for a credit of 112·5 million roubles* (New Delhi: 1961).

[3] For the year 1967–8 the Bhilai plant exported goods valued at 280 million rupees to more than 37 countries.

[4] For the text of the agreement see *Agreement between the government of India and the government of the USSR for the establishment of an integrated Iron and Steel Works* (New Delhi: 1955).

Union was not in the picture, they were not interested in building a state-owned steel plant in India. In fact, negotiations dragged for two years without much progress. But, within five months of Soviet agreement, the West Germans agreed in June 1955 to construct a plant at Rourkela; and eight months later, the English closed the triangle and undertook to build a third plant at Durgapur. Unfortunately, for the English and the Germans, there was a natural temptation to compare the three mills. Comparisons were almost certain to be disadvantageous to the English and Germans because the Russians had chosen the least complex of the three plants. The steel products at Bhilai were less sophisticated in nature, the technical requirements were less demanding and the skills and the machinery needed were therefore less complex. The Bhilai plant produced only merchant steel and rails. The Russians demonstrated their competitive spirit from the moment they announced their willingness to build the steel plant. They assigned their best people to the project. Not only did they catch the English and the Germans unprepared by their speed in working out arrangements, but they offered credit terms that were significantly more favourable. As opposed to an interest rate of 4·5 per cent to 6·3 per cent and a repayment period that had to be extended periodically, the Russian loan was at 2·5 per cent and was repayable over a twelve-year period to begin only one year after the delivery of the equipment. The Russian willingness to accept repayment in rupees generated a far more favourable reaction than the western insistence to be repaid in convertible currency.[1]

The Indians were also pleased by the speed with which the Russians had sent their own technicians home and brought in Indian replacements. The total number of foreigners involved in operating the one-million-ton plant—whose capacity had been expanded to 2·5 million in 1962 and 3·5 million in May 1965—had been reduced from 37 in 1963 to 21 in early 1965.

The Russians also endeared themselves to the Indians because of their agility and receptivity in the Bokaro affair. In addition to the three plants at Bhilai, Durgapur and Rourkela, the long-range plan for Indian steel called for a fourth plant to be built in Bokaro. The plant would specialize in flat steel products which had hitherto been produced only at Rourkela. Since the United States is the world leader in the production of this type of steel, it was considered only natural that she should be asked to undertake construction of the fourth mill. The Indians also reasoned that this

[1] For details see Nina Makrushina, *The Lights of Bhilai. A Story of Steel Makers of India* (New Delhi: 1965).

would be non-alignment at its best, since the United States would find herself alongside the Soviet Union, West Germany and Great Britain.

Negotiations over Bokaro dragged on for several years. In view of the high construction costs during the first stage—estimated to be 919 million dollars including 512 million dollars in foreign exchange—it came under sharp attack in the United States Congress. Not only was the plant expected to cost about double in capital expenditure in comparison to the three other foreign-built plants, but there were some serious doubts as to the existence of sufficient demand for that much steel and the availability of adequate raw material. There was also a demand by American advisers that the project be built on a turnkey basis, i.e. the Americans construct and operate the plant for a ten-year period. While most Indians agreed that a measure of American stewardship might be wise, they were unable to comprehend the need for such a lengthy period. An active and direct participation, they pointed out, was necessary for the technical development of the country.

There was also reluctance on the part of Washington to use American money to build up state-owned at the expense of privately owned steel.[1] Initially the Indian authorities were adamant on the question; but when it became apparent that the whole project might be shelved, they finally agreed that they would be prepared, if necessary, to set up a semi-private corporation in Bokaro. The proposal, however, came too late. Despite the plea of Ambassador J. K. Galbraith and President Kennedy, an American steel mission recommended that the project should not be supported. Rather than force an awkward vote on the issue in the United States Congress, India decided to withdraw the request in order to avoid 'further embarrassment to administrations of both the countries'.[2]

Once again, it was the Russians who seized the initiative. Within a few months of the Indian withdrawal of the request for American assistance, the Soviet Union agreed to build the project.

The first stage of the project was intended to produce 1·5 million tons of ingot and would have a built-in provision for expansion to produce four million tons ultimately.[3]

[1] See B. Maheshwari, 'Bokaro: The Politics of American Aid', *International Studies* (July–October 1968), pp. 113–80; see also William A. Johnson, *The Steel Industry of India* (Massachusetts, Cambridge: 1966).

[2] The *New York Times* of 5 September 1965 reported that Mr Nehru's 'letter prompted a mixture of relief and regret among administration officials'.

[3] O. P. Mehrotra, *Hardware Heavy Equipments Plant help India*(New Delhi: 1968).

It is, however, important to note that the Indians finally had to agree that the Bokaro plant would be designed and built on a turnkey basis after all. Their efforts to obtain a more active and direct participation did not succeed; and their proposal to make an economy of one billion rupees was not accepted.[1]

Nevertheless, the Russian offer had some attractive aspects. In the first place, they prepared a set of revised plans that called for a smaller expenditure in foreign aid. Under the reorganized plan, the Russians agreed to lend India 210 million dollars for the first stage of construction. This was considerably less than the 512 million dollars in foreign exchange that the Americans were expected to lend under the original plan. The revised Russian plan to spend less foreign exchange was made possible by the Russian decision to rely on Indian resources. In fact, more than half the equipment was expected to be supplied by the different Indian industries.[2] The principal source of supply was to be the Heavy Engineering Corporation Ltd at Ranchi, and the machine tool project sponsored and financed by Russia and Czechoslovakia.[3] The use of Ranchi plant to outfit Bokaro was a good idea; if the equipment proved to be of good quality, the Russians would be able to complete the erection of two industrial monuments with a single effort. Thus, not only would Bokaro be built with minimum expenditure of foreign funds, but it would finally provide outlet facilities for Ranchi.

OIL

The second largest area of Soviet economic activity in India is in the field of petroleum drilling and refining. Here too the Russians have been successful in the over-all performance of developing a vital public sector industry and diminishing the economic power of western industries. Until they came on the Indian scene, a closely co-ordinated cartel of three western companies determined oil prices and products in India.[4] They purchased in convertible currency crude oil from their parent companies in the Middle East, shipped it (often in their own tanks) to India, processed it in their refineries and sold it at inflated prices through their own elaborate distribution facilities. This complete control effectively

[1] *The Statesman's Weekly* (14 May 1966).   [2] O. P. Mehrotra, *op. cit.*
[3] See K. Gopalkhrishnen, *Heavy Machine Building Plant, Ranchi* (New Delhi: 1965).
[4] The companies involved were Standard Vacuum Oil Company, California Texas Oil Corporation and Burma Shell.

reduced competitive threats from either outside or internal organizations, since the members of the cartel refused to process any foreign product in their refineries or distribute them through their gasoline stations. Since no real effort was made by western companies to find oil in India, there was generally no alternative but to import oil. During the first two five-year plans, for instance, India had to import oil and oil products worth about a billion dollars (before devaluation), i.e. 11·7 per cent of all the capital investments in the public sector during these years.[1]

For a nation which was continually faced with chronic deficits in its balance of payments, and whose oil deposits had not been seriously explored, this was regarded as an onerous expenditure for the Indian economy. Therefore, when Soviet interest in Indian economic development became increasingly apparent in 1955, the Nehru government took the initiative of seeking Soviet assistance to overcome the stranglehold of the western oil companies. A team of Soviet oil experts, despatched by the Soviet authorities, arrived in India. After five months' exhaustive study of the existing geological survey materials and visits to prospective areas, the Soviet experts came to the conclusion that India possessed considerable oil reserves. And within a short period of time big gas and oil deposits were found in Cambay (1958), Ankleshwar, Kalol and Rudrasagar (1960), providing, according to all calculations, a potential of six million tons of oil a year. By 1960, the eight oil fields in these areas were in fact supplying one-third of India's needs, and by 1966 it was estimated that at least 800 million barrels of oil (including natural gas) which, valued at import parity, would amount to close to 1·5 billion dollars' worth of oil, were being supplied.

Soviet contribution to the construction of oil refineries was also significant. In addition to the building of a public sector refinery in Gauhati with Rumanian help, two of them—one in Baurani and the other in Koyali—have been constructed with the economic and technical assistance of the Soviet Union. Both the refineries have the rated annual capacity of three million tons.[2]

The Russians also rendered valuable assistance in setting up a state-owned network for the distribution and the sale of oil products in the country. In 1960, they offered to supply crude oil at 0·25 dollar a barrel below the posted industry price, making it possible for the state-owned corporation to establish its own network. The corporation's share in the home market was about 30 per cent by 1968.

[1] M. Bogdanchikov, 'Soviet assistance for oil industry', *East European Trade* (January 1965). [2] V. Bolshakov, *Soviet–Indian Economic Co-operation* (New Delhi: 1968).

E

Thus, there does not appear to be any doubt that 'the development of the petroleum industry in the public sector is largely the result of Soviet assistance'.[1]

The Soviet intervention in the oil industry has given an additional advantage to India. It has made it possible for the country to receive competitive bids. The Russians' offer to supply crude oil at 0·25 dollars a barrel below the posted industry price forced the western oil companies to lower their prices by about 0·27 dollar a barrel, 0·2 dollar less than the Russian bid. This meant a revenue loss to the firm and a gain to India of 18 to 31 million dollars a year.[2]

In the case of refineries, too, the Soviet intervention was advantageous to India. When the Indian determination to continue constructing refineries became increasingly apparent, the western companies, realizing the seriousness of the situation, began to make counter proposals which, from the cost angle, were even more attractive than the Russian offers. For example, Phillips Petroleum Company at Baitesville, Oklahoma, won the right to build the refinery for the Indian Government at Cochin at a planned capacity of 2·5 million barrels at 34 million dollars—26 million dollars less than the cost of the Russian refineries at Koyali.[3]

Steel and oil are not the only sectors in which Soviet assistance was extended to India. There are many other important sectors which have been or are being constructed with Soviet financial and military aid. There are three projects in the field of heavy machines—heavy machinery building plant (Ranchi), coalmining machinery plant (Durgapur) and heavy electrical plant (Harwar)—which when completed will provide the main bases of India's self-reliant industrial growth. There are four Soviet-aided thermal or hydro-electric power stations which meet the demand of power for agricultural and industrial loads. And there are— just to name a few more—the surgical instruments plant in Madras, the synthetic drug project in Hyderabad, the antibiotic plant in Rishikesh, and the ophthalmic glass project in Durgapur.

According to the calculations that have been made, the Soviet-aided projects, once completed, will produce annually 9·2 million tons of coal, 6·5 million tons of oil, 6·4 million tons of iron ore, refine 6·5 million tons of oil, generate over 3 million KW of electricity, produce 4·9 million tons of steel, 125,000 tons of metallurgical, mining, oil drilling and other heavy equipment, hydraulic and thermal turbines and generators to a

[1] These were the words used by Humayun Kabir who was the Minister of Petroleum and Chemicals, see *Soviet–Indian Co-operation in Oil Industry* (New Delhi: 1966).

[2] Marshall I. Goldman, *Soviet Foreign Aid* (New York: 1964), p. 96.   [3] *Ibid.*, p. 99.

total capacity of 2·7 million KW, a lot of precision instruments, medicines, surgical instruments, etc.[1]

The Soviet contribution to long-term Indian economic development is indeed significant, and it has played a decisive role in the forging of close and meaningful ties between the two countries. This was naturally considered as an important development by most Indians, as it implied not only a general Communist approbation of India's policy of non-alignment, but it also permitted her to decrease her dependence on the West, and thereby successfully attain a balance between the East and the West without being criticized by either of them that she had slidden into the other camp.

[1] O. P. Mehrotra, *op. cit.*, p. 4.

CHAPTER V

MOSCOW–PEKING–DELHI TRIANGLE

(a) *China abandons peaceful coexistence*

The general Communist approbation of India's foreign policy, however, did not last long; for by 1959 it became increasingly evident that Communist China was rapidly veering away from a gradualist and moderate approach in internal as well as external affairs.

Internally, the 'hundred flowers' movement that was launched to generate a free discussion was abruptly ended in 1958. A vigorous programme of political education and Cromwellian conformity was initiated to eradicate doubts and 'erroneous' thoughts that were increasingly in the ascendant among Chinese intellectuals. Top positions in higher educational institutions were allotted to party officials to ensure political and ideological conformity, and a number of senior Communists who had shown some sympathy for liberal ideas were dismissed and expelled from the party.[1]

In the place of the 'hundred flowers', the policy of 'the great leap forward' was launched with great panache. The carefully planned targets announced at the Eighth Party Congress of the Communist party in 1956 were flung aside for fancifully ambitious projects. The five-year goals set out for 1962 were now to be accomplished within one year. In place of doubling industrial production, it was to be multiplied six-and-a-half times. Instead of increasing agricultural output by 35 per cent, it was to be multiplied two-and-a-half times. Steel output of five-and-a-half million tons in 1957 was to be doubled in 1958. Britain was to be surpassed in industrial power within fifteen years and in heavy industry within ten years, reaching an impressive steel target of 48 million tons by 1972.[2] Communism was no longer considered as a distant dream that may come true some time in the remote future, but something which was

---

[1] Among those expelled included the Governor of Chekiang province, the Governor of Chinai province, the Deputy Governor of Anhwei province and the Deputy Minister of Supervision.

[2] For details see Niu Chung-Huang, *China Will Overtake Britain* (Peking: 1959), pp. 28–32.

fast becoming a reality with the rapid introduction of people's communes.[1]

Externally, more and more emphasis was laid on the decisive shift of the international balance of power in favour of the Communist countries, on the unchanging character of United States policy to dominate the world,[2] and on the relevance of 'uninterrupted revolutions' in the developing countries.[3]

But the most striking development in Chinese thinking was perhaps the manifestation of increasing disappointment with the whole phenomenon of nationalist revolutions in the third world. The Chinese leadership seemed to fear that time was not necessarily on the Communist side in the developing areas; and that the new independent governments, established by non-Communist political figures, may stabilize themselves and eventually gravitate back into the western fold. Writing in the anniversary issue of *Hung chi*, Wang Chia-hsiang, a secretary of the Chinese party, voiced impatience with national leaders, warning that they might slide back into the imperialist camp, and in any case never free themselves from imperialist bondage:

The bourgeoisie which is in power in these countries (Asia and Africa) has played to a certain degree a historically progressive role. . . . It may to a greater or lesser degree go part of the way in opposing imperialism and feudalism. . . . But after all, the bourgeoisie is a bourgeoisie. When in power it does not follow resolute revolutionary lines; it oscillates and compromises. Therefore, it is out of the question for these countries to pass to socialism, nor is it possible for them to accomplish in full the tasks of the national democratic revolution. What is more, even the national independence they have achieved will not be secure . . . there may emerge bureaucratic-capitalism which gangs up with imperialism and feudalism. Thus in the final analysis they cannot escape the control and clutches of imperialism.[4]

As an integral part of this general militant line, the non-aligned countries were made an important target of Chinese hostility. The first such country to feel the hot breath of Chinese hostility was Egypt. Nasser was criticized for having embarked on a policy of persecuting Egyptian and

[1] For details see *People's Communes in China* (Peking: 1958).

[2] Yu Choo-Li, 'The Chinese People's Great Victory in the Fight against Imperialism', *Peking Review* (22 September 1959).

[3] Liu Shao-chi, *The Victory of Marxism–Leninism in China* (Peking: 1959).

[4] *Dix glorieuses années* (Peking: 1960), pp. 305–6.

Syrian Communists, and for having manifested serious reservations in regard to the Kassem régime in Iraq which had shown evident signs of pro-Communist orientation.[1] Nasser was also accused of having abandoned the struggle against imperialism, and was warned that the people may have to form a new judgement of them in the light of the new facts'.[2] Indonesia was bitterly attacked for limiting the economic power of overseas Chinese, and was publicly warned that the Chinese Government and the Chinese people would not 'simply look on while their compatriots are being subjected to discrimination and persecution abroad'.[3] With Burma considerable difficulties were raised on the alignment of border between the two countries. The package deal that had been originally proposed by Chou En-lai in 1956, and accepted by the Burmese, was reneged in the summer of 1957. And all the efforts of the Burmese Government in 1958–59, which was 'prepared to go to almost any length within the new set of Communist Chinese terms to settle the difference', were rebuffed.[4]

India, however, was the principal target of Chinese hostility. A number of Indian political parties were accused of fomenting the Tibetan revolt of March 1959, and the Indian Parliament was denounced for interfering in the internal affairs of China.[5] An unusually long editorial appeared in *People's Daily* on 6 May in which, alternating between condescending friendliness and outspoken intransigence, Nehru was criticized for his views on Tibet.[6] For the first time (January 1959) the entire border alignment between India and China was questioned, and in September of the same year, after some border incidents, a formal claim was laid to about 50,000 square miles of what the Indians considered to be a part of their territory.

(b) *Soviet prudence on Sino-Indian differences*

It would be, however, incorrect to conclude from all this that Peking had artificially created problems which were non-existent. For difficulties and problems had in fact existed with almost all Asian nations. The border problems with India and Burma were not new developments, the

[1] *Peking Review* (24 March 1958).   [2] *Ibid.*   [3] *Ibid.* (15 December 1959).
[4] Frank N. Trager, *Burma—From Kingdom to Republic* (London: 1966), pp. 244–5.
[5] *Peking Review* (31 March 1959).
[6] The editorial was entitled 'The Revolution in Tibet and Nehru's Philosophy'. For complete text see *Tibet Documents* (New Delhi: 1959).

overseas Chinese issue had been apparently aggravated by Djarkarta's unilateral decision to limit their economic power in the country. In Laos, the new right-wing government had been forcibly installed; in Pakistan, American military bases had been set up; and the Japanese Government had declined to give diplomatic immunity to the Chinese trade mission under the fourth trade agreement.

All these intractable problems thus existed long before 1958 and were by no means an artificial creation of the Chinese leaders. But during the period of peaceful coexistence, when the Chinese leaders were seeking common ground with other Asian countries, they considered it expedient to remain uncommunicative on these issues. During 1958–59, when signs of belligerence and radicalism were becoming increasingly evident, they allowed these differences to bubble to the surface.

In any event a general feeling of apprehension arose in India about the possible Soviet reaction to the Sino-Indian dispute. For how could the Soviet Union, many argued, remain neutral in a conflict between a Communist and a non-Communist country? Therefore, when the Sino-Indian relations had become particularly tense following the Longju incident in August 1959, it was widely assumed that Moscow would support Peking, thus recreating a common hostile front against India on the same lines as had existed during the first few years after Indian independence. However, to the surprise of many observers, the Soviet leaders adopted a line of neutrality. Through a *Tass* statement of 9 September 1959, the Soviet Government deplored the Sino-Indian dispute, and expressed the hope that it would be settled through peaceful negotiations between the two states. The statement declared:

The Soviet leaders express the conviction that the government of the Chinese People's Republic and the Republic of India will not let the incident further the aim of those who want the international situation not to improve but to degenerate, and aspire not to permit the emergent lessening of tension between states. The same circles express the conviction that both the governments will settle the misunderstanding that has arisen, taking into account their mutual interests in the traditional friendship between the peoples of India and China. This will also help strengthen those forces that are for peace and international co-operation.[1]

Such a view was reiterated by Khruschev personally. Speaking at a meeting of the Supreme Soviet on 31 October, he regretted the incidents

[1] *Pravda* (19 September 1959).

between 'states friendly to us' and stated that 'we would be very happy if there were no more incidents, if the existing frontier disputes were settled through friendly negotiations to the satisfaction of both parties'.[1]

Such an attitude on the part of the Soviet Government was indeed unprecedented; for never since the formation of Communist states in Eastern Europe and the Far East had Moscow adopted a posture of neutrality in any dispute between a Communist and a non-Communist state.

What was it that led the Soviet leaders to adopt such an unusual attitude? Why did they pursue such a non-committal line when it was unobtrusively evident that any public expression of neutrality would only introduce another element of strain in the already aggravated relations with Peking?

It would appear that there were two important considerations that may have led the Soviet Government to adopt such an unusual attitude. First of all, by 1959 Soviet policy towards the non-aligned world had become remarkably successful. By that year, it had not only succeeded in establishing viable economic relations and forging useful political links with most of them, but had successfully disengaged many of them from the West—an important Soviet objective. Naturally, the Soviet Government was reluctant to undo all these achievements—which might have been the case if they had sided with the Chinese on the Sino-Indian border dispute.

Secondly, by 1959, Sino-Soviet differences had bubbled to the surface. A few differences had become evident and there were some indications that China and the Soviet Union had decided to go their different ways. Under the circumstances, therefore, Moscow was unlikely to risk losing its already enhanced prestige among the non-aligned countries in order to appease China, who appeared determined to go her own way. None the less the Sino-Soviet dispute was still in its early stages and Moscow apparently did not wish to take a major step that might further aggravate it.

It is therefore not surprising that the initial Soviet attitude on the Sino-Indian border dispute was that of prudence, and the aim of Soviet diplomacy appeared to be to persuade the two countries to resolve their differences through bilateral negotiations. As China was already a partisan of bilateral talks, much of Soviet diplomatic action was directed towards persuading the Indian decision-makers to meet the Chinese. On 20 January, there had come to Delhi on a two-week visit a distinguished Soviet delegation led by President Voroshilov and which included such important personalities as Kozlov, the first Deputy Chairman of the USSR Council

[1] N. S. Khruschev, *World Without Arms, World Without Wars* (Moscow: 1959), p. 399.

of Ministers, and Mme Ye A Furtseva, a well-known deputy of the Supreme Soviet.[1] The occasion was, in all probability, used to discuss extensively the Sino-Indian differences and to persuade reluctant Nehru to extend an invitation to Chou En-lai to discuss the explosive situation.

That the Soviet intervention was successful is evident from the fact that within a few days after the departure of the delegation (5 February), Nehru invited Chou En-lai for a meeting in New Delhi. It was indeed a major *volte face*.[2]

What led to this unexpected shift in Indian policy? Why did Nehru suddenly decide to meet Chou En-lai when he had so far resisted all such proposals? Although the exact reasons are obviously not known, one could venture to suggest that he did not have much choice. Faced with an aggravating dispute, he could hardly afford to antagonize the Soviet Union; for any development of such a nature would have negated the Indian policy of non-alignment and would have led the Indian decision-makers once again to turn to the West. Furthermore, the categorical refusal by Nehru to meet Chou En-lai unless certain conditions were satisfied was by no means a popular stand in the eyes of many nations, least of all on the part of a nation who had continuously harped on the vital importance of negotiations to resolve intractable international issues. In fact, Peking had already begun to make propaganda capital among the Communist and non-aligned nations by underlining the importance of peace and by stressing the unreasonableness of India.

However, in the prevailing state of public opinion of India—including his own parliamentary party—it was not possible for Nehru to conduct negotiations on a give-and-take basis with Chou En-lai. The political atmosphere was too charged and public opposition had become too strong to permit the government to make any concessions to break the seemingly intractable deadlock. Therefore when Chou En-lai, during his visit to New Delhi in April 1960, proposed the interesting and not too unreasonable bargain of surrendering the Indian claim over the Akshai Chin area in the North-West in lieu of Chinese recognition of the McMahon line, it was rejected. The negotiations failed and the Chinese Prime Minister went back from the Indian capital disappointed, embittered and in a rage—to which he gave vent at a press conference in Khatmandu, where he flew from New Delhi. India's rejection of Chou's proposal was taken

[1] *Hindu* (21 January 1960).

[2] Khruschev came to India a few days later and also discussed the Sino-Indian border differences; see *Hindu* (13 February 1960).

by Peking as a signal for tougher action. It was probably this which led the Chinese decision-makers to precipitate a showdown with India.

The border incidents between the two countries now became more frequent, and verbal attacks more vitriolic. Nehru began to compare Chinese actions on the border 'to the activities of Hitler in the modern age',[1] and the Chinese openly identified Nehru to the 'expansionist philosophy of the Indian big bourgeoisie'.[2]

(c) Resurgence of the Sino-Soviet dispute

Just as this was happening, just as Communist China was pouring a torrent of harsh criticism against the Indian decision-makers, Sino-Soviet relations continued to deteriorate. At first the differences appeared to be of a minor nature. But it soon became apparent that they were serious, relating to the important principles of Marxist theory and practice, to the assessment of the international situation and to the type of strategy and tactics that ought to be adopted by the Communist world in its confrontation with the West. Without delving into the details of the dispute—for much has already been written[3]—it would be important to dwell briefly upon the different views held in Moscow and Peking, since they had an important bearing on Chinese policy towards India and the rest of the third world.

The post-Stalinist leadership argued that the possession of nuclear weapons by Washington and Moscow had made war unacceptable as an instrument of social change. An explosion of a conflict between the super-powers would not any more lead to the advancement of Communism, but to the total destruction of all social systems. Therefore the only way left to achieve the Communist goal of world revolution was through peaceful but competitive coexistence. This peaceful struggle, argued the Soviet leaders, could be successfully won by demonstrating to the outside world that the socialist model of development and distribution could satisfy the material and spiritual needs of humanity far more effectively

[1] Jawaharlal Nehru, *Prime Minister on Sino-Indian Relations* (New Delhi: 1962), p. 167.
[2] Editorial in *People's Daily*, *More on Nehru's Philosophy in the light of Sino-Indian Boundary Question* (Peking: 1962).
[3] For background information about the Sino-Soviet dispute see Donald S. Zagoria, *The Sino-Soviet Conflict 1956–61* (New York: 1966); François Fejto, *Chine–URSS. La Fin d'une Hégémonie* (Paris: 1964); François Fejto, *Chine–URSS. Le Conflit* (Paris: 1966); W. E. Griffith (analysed and documented), *The Sino-Soviet Rift* (London: 1964).

than the economic system existing in the West. And the only way this would be convincingly done would be through the continuous development of the socialist economies, until the entire bloc was to become the most powerful force in the world, at which point the ultimate offensive against the capitalist West could be effectively launched. That the Communist world could economically surpass the capitalist countries of the West, that it could eventually cause the continual 'multiplication of benefits' for its citizens, leaving the West far behind, of all this the Soviet leaders were convinced. They were convinced because the stimuli for economic growth, in their view, were built in within the socialist society. Accordingly, the role of the third world in this scheme of things could only be secondary in view of their economic backwardness, for premature Communist revolutions in these countries would only undermine the original Communist objective of becoming more powerful than the western world, since the Soviet Union and other advanced Communist countries would have to provide these countries with a massive amount of economic assistance, instead of concentrating on the task of developing their own socialist economies.

Therefore, in the Soviet view, the objective of the Communist bloc in the third world countries should be to encourage them to develop their non-capitalist economies under the leadership of the national bourgeoisie; and the diplomatic power and, to some extent, the economic strength of the bloc ought to be used for the specific purpose of keeping these countries disengaged from the West. In short, what the Soviet Union was suggesting was a holding operation in the third world while the battle of world revolution was conducted by the socialist countries.

The Chinese Communists rejected these arguments. That the socialist countries should concentrate on the rapid development of their economies, that they should strive significantly to improve the standard of living of their citizens was, without any doubt, an understandable objective which obviously merited considerable and sympathetic attention on the part of all Communist governments. But to identify all this with the primordial Communist objective of world revolution was the height of national chauvinism which had no place in the international Communist movement. And further, to suggest that the economic advancement of the Communist world would automatically, spontaneously and inevitably rally the rest of the world around the Communist flag, they considered, was patently absurd, as there was no historical evidence to suggest that such an evolution had ever taken place in the past. If anything, history was full of numerous examples pointing in the opposite direction—the direction of violence and change. Furthermore, even if such a line of argument was accepted, there was no guarantee that the 'capitalist-imperialist' forces, though a small minority, would not use force to prevent such an evolution towards Communism. Accordingly, these forces must be defeated by a continuous offensive against them, first of all in areas where they were most vulnerable. And in the Chinese Communist view, the areas where they were most vulnerable was the under-developed world which is in the midst of important revolutionary upheavals where a faithful application of the Chinese strategy would inevitably lead to the defeat of the western world.

Undoubtedly, the differences between Moscow and Peking were serious. By the early sixties, it became apparent that they were fast escalating into a dispute spreading in all directions and on all points. Obviously, this was a serious situation as the principal and powerful countries of the Communist bloc were involved, and there was now a distinct danger that with the further degeneration of the dispute, the entire international Communist movement, which had so far maintained —with minor exceptions—a monolithic unity, might become seriously divided and thereby lose its effectiveness on the international scene. And once this would happen, it was obvious that the two Communist giants would lose one of the important instruments that they had ruthlessly used in order to attain some of their foreign policy objectives.

Therefore, in order to forestall the development of such an unfavourable situation, which was obviously not in the interst of either of the two countries, a dialogue was opened in 1963 in order to eliminate the differences 'so that we can unite our forces against our common enemy'.[1] But this dialogue which was in the form of an exchange of letters between Moscow and Peking did not improve Sino-Soviet relations. If anything, it only worsened them. And when it became evident that there was really no hope of improvement, the two countries manœuvred to win support among the Communist parties, and to shift the odium of worsening relations to the other side. The ferocity with which the two Communist countries tried to undermine each other's positions was as striking as the ferocity with which they had hitherto indulged in indigestible encomiums underlining their friendship for each other.

[1] *The Polemic on the General Line of the International Communist Movement* (Peking: 1965), p. 65.

(d) *Moscow abandons prudence*

The development of the new situation encouraged the Soviet leaders to abandon their prudence on the Sino–Indian border dispute. Without delving into the substantive issues involved in the conflict, they began to become more critical of Peking's attitude towards India.

In an interview with the Moscow correspondent of the Indian Communist Party's weekly, *New Age*, in November 1960, Khruschev suggested in his flamboyant manner that China's policy was incorrect and compared it with that of the Soviet Government which had given away some of its territory to Iran to settle the border dispute with her southern neighbour.[1] According to Chinese sources, the Central Committee of the Soviet Communist Party had informed the Chinese party in a verbal notification that 'one cannot possibly seriously think that a state such as India which is economically and militarily immeasurably weaker than China would really launch a military attack on China and commit aggression against it'.[2]

In contrast to this attitude towards China, Moscow intensified its economic and cultural relations with India. A few weeks after the *Tass* statement of September 1959, the Soviet Union signed an agreement with India, providing aid for the construction of an oil refinery at Baurani. She extended a little over 115 million rupees of credit for this project at 2·5 per cent interest, with payments to be started twelve months after delivery of the equipment.[3] Also in the same month, an agreement was signed between the two countries to expand the Bhilai Steel Plant and the Ranchi Heavy Machinery Plant, to build a thermal power station and to construct a nuclear power plant.[4] In February 1960, Khruschev himself arrived in India with the obvious purpose of consolidating relations between the two countries. And in June 1960, Moscow and New Delhi signed an oil agreement which provided for Soviet technical collaboration in the exploitation, development and production of oil and natural gas in India.[5]

The number of cultural agreements also increased. By 1960, the Soviet Union had made ten cultural agreements with India.[6] Professor Barghoorn wrote in 1960: 'With the exception of Communist China, India has now

[1] *Link* (15 August 1962).   [2] *People's Daily* (2 November 1963).
[3] For details see *Soviet Indian Co-operation in Oil Industry* (Moscow: 1965), pp. 22–30.
[4] For details see Y. S. Morozov (editor), *op. cit.*   [5] *Oil Co-operation, op. cit.*
[6] *Asian Recorder* (5–11 March 1960), p. 3189.

for several years been the main target of Soviet cultural penetration.'[1]
And with the lessening of Soviet economic and cultural ties with China,
India became perhaps the number one target of Soviet cultural diplomacy.[2]

Irked by the Soviet attitude towards India, Communist China raised
the whole question at the conference of the eighty-one Communist
parties held in Moscow in November 1960.[3] Teng Tsao-Ping, the
General Secretary of the Chinese Communist Party, is reported to have
stated that the Sino-Soviet dispute actually began with the publication
of the *Tass* statement of 9 September 1959. Said Teng Tsao-Ping:

It all began when the *Tass* statement on the Sino-Indian border dispute
was published on 9 September 1959. Long before the appearance of that
statement, we had repeatedly informed the Soviet comrades about the
true facts of the Sino-Indian border incident and asked the Soviet comrades to refrain from actions that might add to China's difficulties. But
the Soviet comrades hastily published that statement in which they
expressed their regret without delving into who was right and who was
wrong and without waiting for the opinion of the Chinese comrades.
The said statement was employed by the imperialists and reactionaries for
nefarious purposes. But the Soviet comrades refused to admit to this day
that it was the *Tass* statement which revealed to the whole world that
there are differences between China and the Soviet Union.[4]

The General Secretary of the Chinese Party bluntly criticized Khruschev
for his unfriendly remarks about China's behaviour on the border
question. He said:

We are obliged to note . . . Comrade Khruschev's interview on 7 November with a correspondent of the *New Age* weekly in which he rebuked
China; and other measures undertaken by Soviet comrades indicate that
they are in fact siding with Nehru, a bourgeois statesman, that they are
opposing China, a fraternal socialist country. . . . It stands to reason that
this incorrect attitude and these incorrect actions of the Soviet comrades
cannot facilitate, and in fact did not facilitate an improvement in Sino-
Indian relations. On the contrary they only caused elation among the
imperialists and enabled the Indian bourgeoisie to utilize these differences
for their purpose of complicating Sino-Indian relations. The result was

---

[1] Frederick C. Barghoorn, *The Soviet Cultural Offensive* (Princeton: 1960), p. 195.
[2] For details see Peter Sager, *Moscow's Hand in India* (Berne: 1966).
[3] *Link* (15 August 1962), p. 73.   [4] *Ibid.*

that Nehru's attitude on the Sino-Indian border issue became more adamant and Comrade Chou en-lai failed to reach a compromise in the negotiations during his second visit to Delhi.[1]

The Soviet reply to this was that the Chinese leaders were making serious mistakes in identifying Nehru, Sukarno and other Afro-Asian nationalist leaders with the imperialists, that they had embroiled themselves in an unnecessary quarrel with India, and that, having done so, they wanted the Soviet Union to come to their rescue and 'intimidate India with rockets'.[2]

Some of the other Communist parties who were, on the face of it, less involved in a controversy with Communist China also rebuked the latter for having chosen the wrong moment for raising the dispute. The French Communist leader, Maurice Thorez, for example, stated at the meeting:

We were alarmed by the tense situation created between the two big Asian States, both of whom constitute a part of the socialist camp. We deplore that an occasion was given to Eisenhower to obtain a welcome in India which he would not have received in other circumstances.[3]

However, when the Chinese troops launched their massive attack on India on 20 October 1962, Moscow made a *volte face* and squarely sided with the Chinese. In an editorial on 25 October 1962, *Pravda* denounced the McMahon line as a line imposed by the imperialists and approved the Chinese cease-fire proposals.[4]

What were the reasons for this sudden and unexpected change? Was it because the pro-Peking elements had suddenly gained the upper hand, or was it because the Soviet leaders, seriously embroiled in the Cuban crisis, were eager to avoid a showdown with Peking at that time?

Whatever might have been the reasons for such a radical change, one thing was certain: many in India were deeply disappointed. A number of members of Parliament reacted strongly against the Soviet reaction to the dispute. Even E. V. Baliga, President of the National Council of the Indo-Soviet Cultural Society, deplored the stand taken by the Soviet Union.[5]

The Indian Government, however, did not give up hope that Moscow might change its attitude once the Cuban crisis had subsided. Therefore,

[1] *Link* (15 August 1962), p. 73.   [2] *Ibid.*   [3] *L'Humanité* (10 January 1963).
[4] *Pravda* (25 October 1962). For English text see *Soviet News* (25 October 1962).
[5] *Background* (10 December 1962), p. 2.

despite the existence of general disappointment in the country, Nehru avoided criticizing Moscow, and actually went to the extent of stating that he understood Soviet difficulties on the question. He said:

The Soviet Union has been, as the house knows, consistently friendly to us. It has been put in a very difficult position in this matter, because they have been and are allies of China, and hence the embarrassment to them as between a country with which they are friendly and a country which is their ally. We have realized that and we do not expect them to do anything which would definitely mean a breach over there. It is not for us to suggest to any country. But we have had their goodwill all along, even very recently, and that is a consolation to us and we certainly have that in the future.[1]

On 5 November, however, the Soviet Government reverted to its original neutralist line. In an editorial on the border question, *Pravda* now maintained a complete silence about the McMahon line and no longer extended support to the Chinese cease-fire proposal. A simple appeal was made to both the sides instead to agree to a cease-fire and to discuss the whole question without imposing any conditions.[2]

The Soviet Government, however, was reluctant to give any significant military assistance—including the squadron of MIGs it had promised —during the explosive period in 1962, for this would have been a clear sign of their sympathy for India. But they made it clear to the Indian Government that Moscow would not raise any serious objections to India's seeking assistance from Washington provided this would not lead to any military alliance between India and the United States and provided not much propaganda capital would be made of it.[3]

With the further aggravation of the Sino-Soviet dispute, Moscow even renounced its posture of neutrality, and began openly to criticize China for her attitude towards India. At the Italian Communist Party Congress, held in December 1962, F. Koslov criticized the Chinese party of what he called 'adventuristic position' on the Sino-Indian border conflict. 'Those who are certain of their historic position', he said, 'have no need to play with fire and endanger all the achievements of civilization'.[4] In a

[1] Indian Ministry of External Affairs, *Prime Minister on Chinese Aggression* (New Delhi: 1962), p. 87.

[2] *Pravda* (5 November 1962).

[3] John K. Galbraith, *Ambassador's Journal. A Personal Account of the Kennedy Years* (London: 1969), p. 458.   [4] *New York Times* (4 December 1962).

series of articles in August 1963, *Pravda* denounced Chinese aggression against India, and lashed out at Peking's failure to seek a peaceful settlement of the Sino-Indian border dispute.[1] On 15 February 1964, Suslov, in his report to the plenary session of the Central Committee of the Soviet Communist Party, also condemned Chinese policy towards India, and viewed it as having 'rendered a great service to imperialism and done grave harm to the national liberation movement, the progressive forces of India and the entire front of the anti-imperialist struggle'.[2] He further added:

No matter how the Chinese leaders try belatedly to justify their behaviour, they cannot escape the responsibility of the fact that by their actions, they essentially helped extreme circles of imperialism thereby aggravating an already complicated and dangerous situation in this world.[3]

At the same time, the Soviet Union stepped up aid to India and concluded a number of agreements covering specific projects. The most important economic agreement was the Soviet accord in January 1965 to construct the Bokaro Steel Plant,[4] which the United States Government had agreed to build but was forced to renounce later because of internal political pressure. It was, however, in the military field that the tempo of Soviet aid was accelerated. Abandoning their policy of prudence on the issue of military aid, the Soviet Union sent all types of armed equipment needed for mountain warfare, agreed to establish factories to manufacture MIG 21 jet fighters, and made available ground-to-air missiles, light tanks, mobile and fixed launching installations and radar equipment which could be used on any part of the Indian frontier. By May 1964, the total military aid emanating from Moscow—130 million dollars— was greater than the aid that was given by the United States during the same period.[5] And in September 1964, India received a new pledge of 140 million dollars under which the Russians agreed to supply 44 MIG 21s, 50 ground-to-air missiles, about 70 light tanks, 6 submarines and an assortment of various infantry weapons.[6] To finance this, the Russians provided a ten-year loan at 2 per cent.

[1] *Pravda* (10 and 13 August 1963).   [2] *Ibid*. (3 April 1964).   [3] *Ibid*.
[4] *Supra*., pp. 88–89.   [5] *New York Times* (13 May 1964).
[6] *Ibid*. (4 August 1965); also see *Link* (20 September 1964).

Chapter VI

THE SOVIET DISENGAGEMENT

It is thus evident that within the general framework of Soviet diplomacy in Asia, India had acquired an important position. In fact, one could venture to suggest that she had by 1964 gained a position of centrality. The quantum of economic and military assistance emanating from Moscow had indeed become considerable; and the political encouragement she had begun to receive to attain some of her vital foreign policy objectives was as striking as the absence of such assistance from the United States and Great Britain.

What were the reasons that led the Soviet decision-makers to adopt such a policy? Why did they focus their prime attention on a nation whose firmly established leadership had often underlined its punctilious fidelity to non-Communist causes, and whose political institutions were more approximate and more comparable to liberal Europe than that of the socialist countries?

India's large size, abundant population and important strategic location must have contributed to the enhancement of Soviet interest in the country. For it is evident that any nation possessing such characteristics is bound, in the long run, to exercise a much greater influence in international affairs than most nations whose relative smallness excludes such a possibility. India furthermore was economically more developed than the other countries of Asia. Apart from possessing a very considerable railway system and a rapidly developing infrastructure, she has a cotton textile industry which produces more than seven billion yards of cloth a year (including handloom production), a jute industry which produces over a million tons of jute cloth a year, a steel industry which produces about six million tons of steel a year, and a rapidly growing chemical, engineering and oil industry. Admittedly in relation to the country as a whole the production is tiny; but considering the rapidity with which the industries are developing, there is a good chance that within the next one or two decades she might acquire a reasonably good industrial status.

Politically too, India had shown striking signs of stability and maturity. Despite the continuous rumblings of discontent that were often discernible on the Indian economic and political landscape, the country did not experience any massive eruptions, and did not manifest any tendency to institute violent changes in her political leadership, as was the case in most of the developing countries. Since her political independence in 1947, she had displayed a remarkable continuity and stability. The Congress party, through the years, had developed effective grass roots within the country which the other parties, including the Communists, were unable to uproot, notwithstanding the unavoidable economic and social discontent that surged up from time to time.

In the field of foreign affairs too, India had acquired an important status. The policy of non-alignment, so sedulously developed by Nehru, had given her a unique moral and political stature; and on a number of occasions she had effectively performed revolutionary as well as mediatory functions in many areas of the world. For the Indonesian nationalists, struggling for their national independence, Nehru had mobilized world opinion against Holland. During the Korean War, he had performed the useful and important function of keeping the belligerents informed of the views and intentions of each other. And at the Geneva Conference of 1954, his delegation had played an important, though indirect, role which finally culminated in the conclusion of political and military agreements on Vietnam.

All this did not escape the attention of Moscow. For notwithstanding the revolutionary proclivities of the Soviet leaders, their escalated dispute with China and their firmly established stature in the world had led them to respond favourably to the few Asian countries who had successfully maintained an element of stability in their political systems. India, who was at loggerheads with China, being one of them, had naturally become an important objective of Soviet diplomacy.

But by the middle sixties, a whole gamut of new factors diminished the importance of India. First of all, she had ceased to carry any major weight in international affairs. The humiliating defeat that China had inflicted on her during the Sino-Indian conflict of 1962 was a brutal exposure of her weaknesses and her inability to defend her interests and security. For the first time, it became evident that she was unable to withstand an attack from a nation which was approximately her size, and which had a similar level of economic and political growth; and it was also for the first time that India felt the real necessity of seeking urgent and important military support from the western nations whom she had hitherto viewed with considerable scepticism. The impact of such a disaster was even more striking on many Asian nations; for many of them, impressed by Chinese military strength, had begun to adopt a cautious attitude towards India. At the Colombo conference of non-aligned countries in December 1962, for example, Ceylon, Burma, Indonesia and Ghana, hitherto great friends of India, were careful not to commit themselves to one side or the other, while serious doubts became evident in Nepal, Sikkim and Bhutan about India's ability to shield them against China.

Secondly, the internal Indian situation had also considerably deteriorated, particularly after the death of Nehru. No longer was India as stable as she had been during the Nehru epoch; and no longer could one assert with any certainty that she would be able to maintain continuity as she had done during the preceding period. Fissiparous tendencies had become rampant, social discontent had acquired a more intense character, the Central Government had become weak, and the right-wing forces inside the Congress party showed signs of asserting themselves, while the Communist movement, deeply riven, had considerably declined in political strength.

(a) *The new Soviet response*

For the Soviet Union, which was anxiously seeking an effective counter-balance to the rising Chinese influence in the area, the Indian external performance and internal developments must have been a source of great concern and disappointment.

But what could the Soviet leaders do? How could they respond to the new situation? They could hardly allow the Indian situation to degenerate any further, in view of the fact that the deeply riven Communist movement was in no position to seize power; and they could scarcely permit the right-wing forces to take over the reins of power, considering the disastrous effect it would have had not only on Indo-Soviet relations, but on the over-all Asian situation. At the same time, considering the manner in which the Indian situation had evolved, they could hardly rely exclusively on India, as they had so far done, to serve as an effective counter-balance to China.

The Soviet response to this situation was indeed dextrous. On the one hand, she actively intervened to strengthen India externally, and forestall the swinging of the Indian political pendulum to the right. Important military assistance was continued and considerable efforts were deployed to use its economic and political power to support those elements within the Congress party which were determined to carry out Nehru's policies.

On the other hand, with the downfall of Khruschev, who was the real architect of excessive Soviet involvement in India, the new Soviet leaders adopted a remarkably subtle policy of extricating themselves from a position of immoderate involvement in any one country which was not under their direct control; and strove to develop relations with all nations who had successfully manifested a measure of assertiveness in international affairs. There was Japan with her vital economic power with whom political and economic relations were developed. There was Indonesia with her vast population, strategic location and important natural resources with whom, notwithstanding the military *coup d'etat* of September 1965 that resulted in the total decimation of the Communist party, important relations were maintained. And there were Iran, Turkey and Malaya, allies of the western world, who had become important objects of Soviet diplomacy.

The pursuit of such a line was not only a striking example of the growing sophistication that had become increasingly evident in Soviet diplomatic behaviour, but was perhaps an important sign of a general consensus that such a line, under the existing circumstances, was perhaps the only effective way to safeguard Soviet national interest and, at the same time, aggrandize Soviet influence.

(b) *Moscow develops relations with Pakistan*

Perhaps the most significant development in this direction, so far as India was concerned, was the Soviet decision to forge close ties with Pakistan. Just as there were a number of factors that had led the Soviet leaders to jettison their special relations with India, there were a number of particular developments that catalysed their decision to turn their sights on Pakistan.

In the first place, the Pakistan leaders had begun to show, in the early sixties, signs of re-examining their relations with the outside world, as it had become utterly evident that none of the foreign policy objectives—for which they had made important concessions to the West—had been attained. Notwithstanding their political and military alliance with the western countries, they had been unable to obtain unconditional and complete support from the United States on the Kashmir issue—an issue that had dominated the nation's foreign policy since her creation in 1947.

Admittedly, there is evidence to suggest that the western nations were sympathetic to Pakistan's point of view, but it would be none the less difficult to produce conclusive evidence of their total support of all that

Pakistan did and wished to do to attain her objectives in Kashmir. In fact, after the exacerbation of Sino-Indian relations in 1959, United States interest in India had considerably increased. The press gave greater coverage to Indian developments on the understandable ground that India was the sole competitor to China. Even the Eisenhower administration, which was the principal architect of forging close political and military ties with Pakistan, agreed to send 29 C–11 flying box car transport planes in June 1960.[1]

It was, however, under the Kennedy administration that a new era in Indo-United States relations was really inaugurated. The new President viewed India as an important and pivotal country in Asia who could eventually constitute an effective bulwark against the expansion of Chinese influence in the area. In fact, considering India's relatively viable economic and political structure, it was even thought that she would make a good 'show place' of what the western world could do in an Asian country.[2]

It is therefore not surprising that in the aftermath of the Sino-Indian conflict of 1962, large-scale military assistance was sent to India.[3] Particularly striking was the fact that, with the escalation of the Sino-Indian dispute, United States interest in resolving the intractable Kashmir problem showed signs of flagging on the ground that it was 'not an essential issue in that part of the world'.[4] Pakistan was particularly aggrieved by the fact that Washington was making a 'special effort' to persuade other members of the Aid-India consortium to match her efforts, whereas in the case of Pakistan 'all sorts of objections were raised'.[5]

When all this became apparent—and this became so in the early sixties—Pakistan began to show signs of cautious disengagement from the West. Economic agreements were signed with some of the socialist countries. Efforts were made to forge close political ties with some of the non-aligned nations. The first major effort was made to normalize relations with India. The over-all political situation in South Asia had

[1] G. W. Choudhury, op. cit., p. 260.

[2] Hindu (16 November 1960); see also Arthur M. Schlesinger jr, A Thousand Days: John F. Kennedy in the White House (Boston: 1965), p. 523.

[3] For details see G. W. Choudhury, op. cit., pp. 266–7.

[4] Statement made to the United States House Foreign Relations Committee by William S. Gaud, Deputy Administrator of Aid. Cited by Z. A. Bhutto, The Myth of Independence (London: 1969), p. 71.

[5] Field-Marshal Ayub Khan, Speeches and Statements, Vol. IV (July 1961–June 1962) Karachi: n.d.), pp. 5–6.

considerably deteriorated. The escalation of the Sino-Indian dispute in 1959 and the presence of Chinese troops in areas not too far away from the Pakistan border generated a feeling of uneasiness in the country. If China was prepared to exercise a pressure on a nation with whom she had developed good ties, what guarantee was there that she would not do the same with Pakistan—a nation who was formally tied to the West? Fearing such a situation, Ayub Khan in May 1959 offered Nehru a plan for joint defence of the sub-continent against external threats. He believed that there was a threat to both India and Pakistan; the two countries should therefore settle their outstanding differences and come to a joint defence arrangement. 'The crux of the whole thing', he said, 'is that Indian and Pakistan forces are at the moment facing each other; if differences between them were resolved, these forces could be released for the job of defending their territories'.[1]

Ayub Khan's offer was, however, turned down. Nehru was reported to have said, in a message sent through the Pakistan High Commissioner in New Delhi, that the question of joint defence did not arise because the approaches of the two countries to world affairs was different.[2] In the face of this rebuff, the Pakistan leader took the decision to normalize relations with China; for he did not wish to confront—in addition to India and Afghanistan—another nation with whom some differences subsisted. This decision was obviously dictated by the worsening situation on the Sino-Indian border, and by the fear that the actual non-demarcation of the frontier between Pakistan and China would inevitably lead to friction between the two countries as had already happened between India and China. In fact some minor incidents had already occurred. Reports of flare-ups on the border between Hunza and Gilgit had appeared in the Chinese press, unidentified planes—presumably Chinese—had intruded into Pakistani territory;[3] and some cattle belonging to Pakistani nationals were seized in certain disputed areas by the Chinese.[4]

Therefore, in order to avoid any further exacerbation of Sino-Pakistan relations, the Ayub government took the initiative of suggesting to Peking, towards the end of 1959, to open negotiations to demarcate the undefined border between the two countries.[5]

---

[1] G. W. Choudhury, op. cit., p. 253.   [2] Ibid., p. 254.

[3] Qutubuddin Aziz, 'Relations between Pakistan and the People's Republic of China' in Latif Ahmad Sherwani et al., Foreign Policy of Pakistan (Karachi: 1964), p. 85.

[4] Mohammad Ayub Khan, Friends not Masters. A Political Autobiography (London: 1967), p. 161.

[5] Ibid.

From the evidence that is available, it would appear that such a démarche placed China on the horns of a dilemma. Although it was naturally eager to keep the door open for any eventual negotiations with Pakistan, and even perhaps use it to obtain border concessions from India, she did not wish to begin formal negotiations,[1] as it was evident that such a step would only further exacerbate Sino-Indian relations. Therefore, while continuing informal talks with Karachi, Peking avoided any formal negotiations. Even when the Pakistan Government submitted detailed proposals in May 1961, it prudently stated that it would submit a detailed reply in the near future.[2]

Such a prudent attitude on the part of China, however, did not last too ɪong, as the situation in the area radically altered, necessitating a change in Peking's attitude towards Pakistan.

Sino-Indian relations, which had in all probability restrained China from seeking an understanding with Pakistan, had worsened as a result of a number of serious border incidents between the two countries. By the spring of 1962, they had come to a point of no return, virtually eliminating all hope of an agreement. The negotiations concerning the border had become completely deadlocked, the clashes had become more frequent, and the whole gamut of relations between the two countries was limited to a simple exchange of harsh diplomatic notes full of mutual recriminations concerning border violations.

It is reasonable to assume that this development probably prompted China to abandon the voluntary and unilateral restraint that she had hitherto imposed on herself so far as the development of her relations with Pakistan were concerned. On 3 May 1962, the governments of Pakistan and China simultaneously announced in their respective capitals that they had decided to negotiate an agreement on the border between China's Sinkiang province and the contiguous areas of Hunza and Gilgit, the defence of which was under Pakistan's control. Since the Sino-Pakistan border involved areas in dispute between India and Pakistan, it was announced that the contemplated border agreement would be of a provisional nature. The communiqué thus stated:

The two sides have further agreed that after the settlement of the dispute

---

[1] Chou En-lai informed the Secretary-General of the Indian Foreign Ministry in July 1961 that China had not begun any formal talks with Pakistan. For details see External Publicity Division, Ministry of External Affairs, *Sino-Pakistan 'Agreement' March 2, 1963, Some Facts* (New Delhi: 1963), p. 15.

[2] Qutubuddin Aziz, *op. cit.*, p. 86.

over Kashmir between Pakistan and India, the sovereign authorities concerned shall reopen negotiations with the Chinese Government regarding the boundary of Kashmir so as to sign the border treaty to replace this provisional agreement.[1]

The formal negotiations began on 12 October 1962 with General N. A. M. Raza, who had successfully negotiated the border agreement with Iran, leading the Pakistan delegation.[2] The Chinese were 'very difficult in the beginning' and produced maps which claimed areas on Pakistan's line of control, but 'eventually they agreed to the actual line of control' as shown on the Pakistan maps as the demarcation line, with certain marginal adjustments.[3]

While the negotiations were under way, a number of important events, closely related to the area, took place having an important bearing on the negotiations. On 20 October, the Sino-Indian war exploded leading to the quick defeat of India. It is reasonable to assume that the unexpected explosion of such an event, and the tragic exposure of India's military weakness, which had generated a good deal of sympathy for India around the world, probably induced the Chinese to bring a rapid conclusion of their negotiations with Pakistan. For by doing so, they could project an image of a reasonable nation, seeking peaceful solutions to some of the ticklish problems.

Thus on the day (27 December 1962) on which Indo-Pakistan talks were to open in Rawalpindi on Kashmir, brought about by western pressure, the governments of Pakistan and China simultaneously announced 'an agreement in principle' on the alignment of the border between Sinkiang and that part of Kashmir controlled by Pakistan.[4]

Detailed negotiations were then opened which finally culminated in an agreement on 2 March 1963, setting forth in detail the description of the border alignment between the two countries.[5] Considering the disputed character of the area between India and Pakistan, the agreement was characterized as provisional pending the final resolution of the status of Kashmir. But the elaborate arrangements that were mutually agreed upon—appointment of a boundary commission and the subsequent setting up of the pillars and the drawing of the protocols—obviously

---

[1] *Peking Review* (11 May 1962).

[2] Mohammad Ayub Khan, *Autobiography*, op. cit., pp. 163–4.

[3] K. Sarwar Hasan (editor), *Documents on Foreign Policy of Pakistan. China, India, Pakistan* (Karachi: 1966), p. 366.

[4] *Ibid.*   [5] *Ibid.*

pointed against the provisional character of the agreement. For it is hardly possible—though legally valid—to undo an effective border agreement which has been in force for a certain period of time.

Upon his return from signing the border agreement in Peking, Foreign Minister Bhutto lauded the settlement for awarding Pakistan some 750 square miles of land containing the salt and grazing grounds, for permitting access to all passes along the Karakarom range, and control of two-thirds of K-2 mountains. A few days later, he added that three-quarters of the peak of K-2 including the summit remained with Pakistan.[1] In the National Assembly on 17 July, the Foreign Minister was able to place particular emphasis on the acquisition of the salt mines of Oprang 'which the people of Hunza and the surrounding territory consider necessary for their needs and for their economic well-being'.[2]

Even before the negotiations on the border questions were concluded, a trade agreement was signed on 5 January 1963 between the two countries. It provided for reciprocal most favoured nation treatment in matters of commerce, trade and shipping. The lists attached to the agreement stated that China would export items like metals, steel products, coal, cement, machinery, chemicals, raw materials and cereals. Pakistan's exports would include jute, jute manufactures, cotton, cotton textiles, leather, sport goods, surgical instruments, chrome ore and newsprint. China was reported to have become the biggest buyer of Pakistani cotton during 1963–64. That is to say 302,000 bales out of Pakistan's total export of 539,000 bales.[3]

Another agreement was reached in the sphere of civil aviation in August 1963, permitting Pakistan International Airlines to fly to Canton and Shanghai. The agreement was criticized by the State Department[4] and led Washington to postpone the granting of a loan of 4·3 million dollars for the improvement of Dacca airport on the ground that it was unwilling to pay for the improvement of facilities which the Chinese airlines might use. Furthermore, it was suspected in Pakistan that the United States had pressured Tokyo not to agree to any amendment to the existing Pakistan–Japanese air accord, which would have enabled Pakistan International Airlines to operate its flight to Japan through China.

[1] W. M. Dobell, 'Ramification of the China–Pakistan border', *Pacific Affairs* (autumn 1964).   [2] K. Sarwar Hasan, *op. cit.*

[3] Khalid B. Sayeed, 'Pakistan and China' in A. M. Halpern, *Policies Towards China. Views from Six Continents* (New York: 1965), p. 228.

[4] Richard P. Stebbins, *The United States in World Affairs 1963* (New York: 1964), pp. 173–4.

In addition to the signing of a number of important agreements, an understanding was also reached on a number of international issues which concerned both or either of the two countries. Peking rallied to Pakistan's point of view on Kashmir by accepting the idea of a referendum. Pakistan continued to support China's admission to the United Nations, and both of them publicly expressed the view that a second Afro-Asian conference ought to be convened.[1]

Perhaps the most striking development in Sino-Pakistan relations was the generation of a wide consensus in Pakistan that a military understanding with China—and against India—had become necessary. On 26 April 1963, the important Pakistani newspaper, *Dawn*, proposed that the Pakistani Government should conclude a military agreement with China and discard her 'faithless Christian allies'.[2] Pakistan Foreign Minister Z. A. Bhutto went even further and, in fact, implied that his country had the protection of China. He said:

This much we know and can say that if, God forbid, we should be involved in a clash with India, that is, if India were, in its frustration, to turn its guns against Pakistan, the international position being what it is, Pakistan would not be alone. An attack by India on Pakistan would no longer confine the stakes to the independence and territorial integrity of Pakistan. An attack by India on Pakistan would also involve the security and territorial integrity of the largest state of Asia.[3]

Two days after Bhutto's speech, the Press Association of Pakistan circulated a news item announcing that Pakistan would seek the assistance of Chinese experts for training in guerilla warfare.[4] And in Peking, the Chinese Government assured a visiting Pakistan delegation that China would be ready to give 'all possible help' and material support to Pakistan 'at all times'.[5]

The development of such a situation must have been viewed with great concern by the Soviet leadership; for it was apparent that the forging of Sino-Pakistan ties not only outflanked India, but made it possible for China to establish effective foothold on the sub-continent.

Therefore, in order to forestall any further orientation in this direction, important efforts were deployed to forge closer ties with Pakistan. The

[1] *Peking Review*, No. 9 (28 February 1964).
[2] *Dawn* (26 April 1963).   [3] S. Sarwar Hasan, *op. cit.*
[4] H. Ray, 'Sino-Pakistan Relations', *International Spectator* (22 November 1966), p. 1564.
[5] *Ibid.*, p. 1565.

latter was by no means averse to Soviet overtures. On the contrary, forging of closer ties with Moscow would give her a number of distinct advantages. For one thing, it would permit the Pakistan decision-makers to diversify their relations, thus making it possible for them to acquire an important element of manœuvrability in foreign affairs of which they had hitherto deprived themselves on account of their excessive dependence on the United States. For another, it would make it possible to break the barrier that India had successfully erected between Pakistan and the Soviet Union, and thereby open numerous possibilities of exercising pressure eventually to diminish Soviet commitment to India.

Although some minimal contacts had already been established between the two countries in the early sixties,[1] effective signs of viable normalization however became evident in 1964 and 1965. In 1964, a cultural agreement was concluded, visits were exchanged, and economic relations were developed; favourable articles, praising Pakistan's foreign and economic policies, also began to appear in the Soviet press. In 1965, Ayub Khan arrived in Moscow on an eight-day visit. This was the first time that the head of the Pakistan State was visiting the Soviet Union, and the occasion was fully used to have an extensive exchange of views which resulted in the partial removal of misunderstanding that had plagued the relations between the two countries.[2] The occasion was also used to sign agreements on trade, economic co-operation and cultural exchange. The economic agreements were important in so far as the Soviet Union agreed to assist Pakistan in implementing thirty major development projects during the third five-year plan period, including steel plants, power plants, radio communications, sea ports and air fields.[3]

(c) *Soviet neutrality in the Indo-Pakistan conflict*

Undoubtedly all these agreements were important signs of the new Soviet approach to Pakistan. But the principal development so far as India was concerned was the slow and subtle Soviet disengagement from a position of open partisanship for India on intractable issues that racked Indo-Pakistan relations. This became apparent during the Indian President

[1] For details see Mohammad Ahsen Chaudhri, 'Pakistan's relations with the Soviet bloc', *Asian Survey* (September 1966), pp. 492–500.

[2] For details see Mohammad Ayub Khan, *Autobiography op. cit.*, pp. 168–74.

[3] Kurt London (edited), *New Nations in a Divided World* (New York: 1964), p. 218.

Radhakrishnan's visit to the Soviet Union in September 1964. On this occasion—unlike previous high-level visits—the concluding joint communiqué produced no mention of Kashmir, and laconically stated that 'the territorial disputes between states should be solved by peaceful methods'.[1] During Prime Minister Shastri's visit in May 1965, the Soviet leaders avoided taking a pro-Indian stand on the Kashmir and the Runn of Katch disputes, and expressed the view that the 'Soviet people would like the two countries to settle their border dispute and other disputes peacefully, and all prerequisites for this are there'.[2] Two days later, Kosygin noted that only imperialists could benefit when 'liberated states quarrelled',[3] while the joint communiqué omitted specific reference both to Kashmir and the Kutch issues, and declared elliptically that disputes 'must be solved by way of peaceful talks and the use of force to settle disputes is impermissible'.[4]

By adopting the new line, the Soviet Union succeeded in subtly disengaging herself from the Indo-Pakistan dispute in which she had overly embroiled herself in the middle fifties. But this disengagement could not be likened to the policy of contemptuous disengagement and indifference which she followed after the independence of the sub-continent; for at that time she did not appear to be interested in forging meaningful relations with either of the two governments, whereas in the mid-sixties she was eager to develop relations with both of them.

The skilful handling of a complicated and rather explosive situation stood the Soviet Government in good stead; for not long after the adoption of this line, it was successful in establishing friendly relations with Pakistan without however generating a serious crisis in Indo-Soviet relations, and without arousing the indignation of sensitive India. This remarkable feat of Soviet diplomacy encouraged the decision-makers to become more ambitious in their objectives in South Asia. Instead of limiting their diplomatic action to the simple task of collaterally forging meaningful links with the two rivals, they moved forward and attempted to bring the two countries together. Evidently the effective advancement of Soviet interests on the sub-continent as well as in the rest of Asia was considered to be closely linked with the amelioration of relations between India and Pakistan. At first, however, the Soviet concern was limited to the simple task of making general statements, stressing the urgency of finding 'a way towards the ending of bloodshed and conflict',[5] and

[1] *Soviet News* (21 September 1964), pp. 133–4.   [2] *Ibid.* (17 May 1965), p. 90.
[3] *Ibid.*
[4] *Ibid.* (20 May 1965), pp. 98–9.   [5] *Pravda* (24 August 1965).

avoiding any action that might lead to conflict. But when the Indo-
Pakistan dispute finally exploded with the outbreak of hostilities in
September 1965, Moscow, while carefully avoiding taking sides, initiated
an important offensive to limit the conflict. Pressure was put on both the
sides not to take any action that might escalate hostilities, and several
objections were raised against the Indian decision to open a new front in
the Punjab area in order to relieve pressure on the Kashmir front.[1] At the
same time, the Soviet Government warned the Chinese, who appeared to
have the intention of keeping the pot boiling,[2] not to exacerbate the
already complicated situation 'as many states might find themselves
drawn into the conflict one by one.'[3]

The Soviet leaders, however, knew that the best guarantee against any
further escalation evidently was to bring a rapid end to the conflict; and
it was to this difficult task that they set their sights.

At the United Nations, they indulged in the long, tense and rather
exacting backstage diplomacy to formulate resolutions for peace on the
sub-continent. In view of the fact that the Soviet and American interests
increasingly converged on the question of peace in the area, there was no
great difficulty in hammering out an acceptable resolution to put an end
to hostilities.

Soviet diplomacy, however, did not limit itself to the task of exercising
co-ordinated pressure—along with the United States—to decrease tension
in the area. Having already established firm relations with the two
countries, it also actively deployed considerable independent and direct
efforts to seek a political solution to the Indo-Pakistan conflict.[4] Informal
diplomatic contacts were established with the leaders of the two countries
in order to impress upon them the vital importance of peace in the area.
Appeals were promptly despatched urging them to 'display realism'
restraint and understanding of the grave consequences of the development of the armed conflict'.[5]

---

[1] Hari Ram Gupta, *India-Pakistan War 1965*, Vol. 2 (Delhi: 1968), p. 217.

[2] The Chinese had sent an ultimatum to India on 16 September demanding the
dismantling of 'all its military works for aggression on the Chinese side'. For details see
Ministry of External Affairs, *Documents on China's Ultimatum to India* (New Delhi: 1966).

[3] *Soviet News* (14 September 1965), p. 113.

[4] So far the Soviet Government had rejected Pakistan's proposal for the creation of a
special four-nation United Nations task force to explore Kashmir and other Indo-
Pakistan problems. It had also passed over in silence the Indian suggestion of a joint
Soviet–United States initiative.

[5] *Soviet News* (8 September 1965), p. 101.

(d) *The Tashkent conference*

However, the most important diplomatic move that was made in this direction was the specific proposal to both Ayub Khan and Shastri to meet in the Soviet Union. Kosygin personally offered his good offices to bring an end to the conflict. Stressing the vital importance of negotiations, he said:

One thing is important—to meet and start negotiations. It is important that the guns should become silent and the blood of the two fraternal peoples should cease to flow. Each new day of the armed conflict produces new and complex problems, the solution of which can impose a heavy burden on the peoples of India and Pakistan in the first place.[1]

Admittedly, the Soviet leaders were risking their international prestige by sponsoring an apparently hopeless attempt to settle the impossible. None the less, it was also apparent that should such a conference prove to be successful, Moscow would immeasurably gain from it.

India accepted the Soviet proposal. That she promptly did so is understandable, in view of the fact that there was a general consensus among the Indian decision-makers that the Soviet Union might not protect Indian interests but would not, in any event, go against them.[2] Furthermore, there was a practical reason for India's rapid acceptance of the Soviet proposals: in the face of the Security Council's unanimous resolution requesting the two belligerents to withdraw to the positions they occupied before the commencement of hostilities, India was finding it difficult to retain the vantage position she had occupied in Pakistan-held Kashmir. Perhaps, at Tashkent, the Indian decision-makers calculated, they could force Pakistan to agree to 'certain things' before retreating from their advanced positions.[3]

Pakistan, understandably, was hesitant to accept the Soviet position. For what guarantee was there that the Moscow leaders would go against India with whom they had established firm relations since 1955, and support Pakistan with whom they were still far from developing a viable relationship? Ayub Khan therefore expressed the view that direct negotiations would not be fruitful and proposed that they be carried on within the framework of the Security Council. Evidently, he was hoping to

[1] *Soviet News* (8 September 1965), p. 101.
[2] Kuldip Nayar, *Between the Lines* (New Delhi: 1969), pp. 115–16.
[3] *Ibid.*

neutralize Soviet influence by countering it with that of the United States. But his hopes were dashed to the ground; for it became increasingly apparent that President Johnson was not eager to get directly involved and was indeed not averse to Soviet initiative to arrange the Tashkent meeting. Under the circumstances, the head of the Pakistan State did not have any room for manœuvre, and was thus left with no choice but to cede to the rising Soviet pressure to come to Tashkent.

The Tashkent conference finally opened in difficult circumstances. Both Shastri and Ayub Khan arrived under severe domestic pressure; and the differences between the two nations were obviously too great to be resolved at a conference of such a nature. It was, therefore, not at all surprising that a serious impasse developed in the negotiations and it looked as if they were fast heading towards a breakdown. 'Unless a miracle happens', reported an Indian correspondent, 'the Tashkent conference should end on an unmistakable note of disagreement.... A détente on any basic issue is considered impossible'.[1]

But the miracle did happen. The Soviet determination to make the conference a success led Kosygin to undertake last-minute rescue operations. For fourteen hours, he shuttled back and forth between Ayub and Shastri, trying to convince both of them to agree at least on certain fundamental principles for future bilateral negotiations. It is not excluded that during these dramatic hours, the Soviet Prime Minister exercised considerable pressure on the two leaders; for one cannot otherwise rationally explain the agreement that was thereafter concluded between the two leaders.

The Tashkent declaration, in its most important aspects, announced the accord of the two leaders to withdraw their armed personnel to the position they held prior to 5 August, to exchange prisoners of war, to restore normal diplomatic relations and to settle their differences through peaceful means.[2]

It was indeed a remarkable achievement for Soviet diplomacy; for it had succeeded where the other powers had failed. Because of this remarkable feat, the Soviet Union, it is evident, became an important factor in Indo-Pakistan relations—perhaps more than the other powers.

But if Tashkent was a major diplomatic achievement for the Soviet leaders, it was also an eye-opener for them. The problems that racked Indo-Pakistan relations were too intractable and too forlorn to be resolved

[1] Kuldip Nayar, *op. cit.*, pp. 115–16.

[2] For full treatment of the Tashkent conference see *International Studies* (July–October 1966).

by good offices or through mediatory efforts of a foreign power. The rapidity with which the two nations had quickly set aside the Tashkent agreement, and had nullified the 'Tashkent spirit', was a clear proof of the despairing situation that prevailed in the region. At the two-day bilateral ministerial conference, held in Rawalpindi in March 1966, the basic issues once again raised their ugly heads. Pakistan insisted upon a solution of Kashmir before undertaking other questions, and India refused to budge from her previous position that Kashmir was non-negotiable, although other problems could be resolved. Finally the meeting adjourned with a public promise to reconvene, but it was evident that the prospects were unpromising.[1]

The rapid resurgence of these difficulties must have led the Soviet leaders to the inevitable realization that their fixed objective of actively seeking, through Soviet good offices, a bilateral solution to the Indo-Pakistan conflict was perhaps unattainable under the existing circumstances. Perhaps the continuation of Soviet efforts was considered even hazardous in view of the fact that they would have to stake their prestige, influence and power to resolve what appeared to be a forlorn conflict. At the same time, the Soviet interests in the area were too vital to be ignored; and the neutralization of China's influence on the sub-continent was considered too important to permit them to disengage themselves.

Faced with this intractable dilemma, Soviet diplomacy adopted a new approach. While jettisoning its previous objective of seeking a positive and lasting solution to what was a stubborn conflict, it slowly and subtly moved towards the limited objective of using its power to forestall another violent explosion of the conflict.[2] Such a limited task appeared to be more within the realm of reality, in view of the fact that Moscow exercised powerful influence on the two countries and could probably restrain them from taking any military initiatives.

If the Soviet Union avoided any further over-involvement in the area by formulating limited diplomatic objectives, the continuation of Soviet policy of neutrality in the conflict began, however, to affect Indo-Soviet relations; for it was full of many pitfalls and contained within itself dangerous germs of undermining the very objectives for which it had been originally formulated, namely the goal of increasing influence in the two countries. Having once decided to maintain and develop relations

[1] For details see Richard P. Stebbins, *The United States in World Affairs 1966* (New York: 1967), pp. 217–25.

[2] The joint statement that was issued after Kosygin's visit in May 1969 did not contain any reference to the Tashkent declaration. See *The Statesman's Weekly* (7 June 1969).

G

with both India and Pakistan, Moscow was increasingly obliged, with the aggravation of Indo-Pakistan tension, to adopt policies that vitiated the collateral growth of relations with both of them.

The Soviet decision to give military assistance to Pakistan is a case in point. In the middle sixties, all the Pakistani efforts to obtain military assistance from Moscow were firmly resisted by the Soviet leaders. However, it soon became apparent that the continuous hedging on such an important issue was generating a difficult situation for the Soviet Government.

In the first place, it was leading to a continual manifestation of discontent in Pakistan, thereby creating a situation where the continual growth of Soviet–Pakistan relations was being jeopardized. Obviously the Soviet Government, after having sedulously striven to develop relations with Rawalpindi, did not wish them to be undermined.

Secondly, a continual refusal to give arms to Pakistan permitted the leaders of that country to insist in their negotiations with the Russians that they must, in this case, cease to give military assistance to India. In fact, there were some reports that Ayub Khan, during his visit to Moscow in September 1967, used this argument.[1] Apparently the Soviet leaders were not prepared to accept such a proposal as it would have seriously affected Indo-Soviet relations. It was therefore viewed that the making of a symbolic arms deal with Pakistan would permit them to maintain their bridges with that country, without seriously jolting their relations with India.

Thirdly, it was probably calculated that India's economic and military dependence on Moscow was too great to permit the decision-makers of that country to adopt a different policy from the one they had so far pursued. All the other options that India could have chosen were in fact closed. The Chinese and the Pakistanis were not at all interested—at least at that time—in normalizing their relations with New Delhi; and the United States, considering her involvement in Vietnam, was not prepared to get herself bogged down in the whirlpool of the Indo-Pakistan conflict.

Fourthly, the field of military supplies had been left wide open, following the American decision in 1965 to impose an embargo on supplying arms to India and Pakistan. The Soviet Government probably considered that by giving limited arms aid to Pakistan it could make a greater propaganda capital than by simply concentrating on economic assistance in which Washington's capacity was obviously much greater.

Fifthly, the Soviet Government, in all probability, considered that in

[1] *Times of India* (27 September 1967).

exchange for some arms aid to Pakistan they could persuade the Pakistan Government to close the American military base at Badaber in Peshawar, which was known to be an important link in the chain of electronic communications bases in Iran, Turkey, Thailand, Japan and the Philippines, and which the United States used for monitoring Russian and Chinese military activity.

Sixthly, the Soviet Government, in all probability, desired to bolster the Ayub régime. In Soviet eyes, Ayub had been equated with stability in Pakistan. Conditions of instability in that country would have improved the chances of either pro-Peking Bhutto and/or Bashani or the extreme rightist *Jamaat-il-islami* of taking over power.

So the Soviet stake in a stable régime in Pakistan was therefore great; and the sale of Soviet arms could be interpreted as an important step towards building up Ayub's image in Pakistan, since his régime was constantly under criticism from both the extreme right and the extreme left for its inability to win over the Soviet Union.

A decision thus was taken, during the first few days of July, to give military aid to Pakistan.[1] But, significantly, India was kept in the dark. It was only after the first Karachi press reports came out announcing the agreement that Kosygin, on 6 July, sent a message to Mrs Gandhi vaguely indicating the probability of an arms deal with Pakistan of a kind that would not affect the general military and political balance on the subcontinent.[2]

[1] For details about Soviet military aid to Pakistan see Mohammad Ayoob, 'Soviet arms aid to Pakistan', *Economic and Political Weekly* (19 October 1968).

[2] Kuldip Nayar, *op. cit.*, p. 103.

Chapter VII

CRISIS

(a) *India's reaction to Soviet actions*

The Soviet decision to give arms aid to Pakistan did not fail to create rumblings of discontent in India. In fact, it generated a minor crisis in Indo-Soviet relations. The right-wing political parties vigorously condemned the Soviet decision. The president of the *Jan Sangh* party, for instance, proposed to the Indian Prime Minister to convene an urgent meeting of all parties to evolve a national consensus on the issue.[1] At the same time an angry demonstration was staged outside the Soviet information centre in New Delhi which, because of its disorderly nature, had to be dispersed with tear gas and lathi charge. Some of the leading members of the Congress party were also critical of the Soviet action. The Secretary of the Congress Parliamentary Party, for example, expressed the view that the 'Soviet decision indicated that she attached more importance to friendship with Pakistan for it was strategically placed'.[2]

The Indian Communist movement, already seriously divided as a result of the Sino-Soviet dispute, was also bemused by the new development. Before the parliamentary debate, it was evident that many leaders of the pro-Soviet Communist Party were in fact ready to disapprove of what appeared to be a sudden and rather objectionable shift in Soviet policy in favour of a state that continued to remain a member of SEATO and CENTO. The party's general secretary, Rajeswar Rao, declared on 10 July that 'we are against any which jeopardizes the security of our country'.[3] But the demand of the Swatantra party and other members of the right opposition in the Parliament for a vigorous condemnation of the Soviet Union induced the Communist leaders to oppose the move. In the face of such a situation, they were apparently left with no choice but to rally around the Soviet Union, for any support of the right wing initiative would have only led to a crisis between Moscow and the Communist party of India, which the latter wished to avoid at any cost.

[1] *Times of India* (12 July 1968).   [2] *National Herald* (10 July 1968).
[3] *Times of India* (11 July 1968).

The rival Communist party of India (Marxist), on the other hand, attacked the Soviet policy in its organ, *People's Democracy*, declaring that the old days of 'exclusive Soviet-Indian friendship is gone for ever'.[1]

The attitude of the Indian press was also on the whole critical. While one newspaper regarded it 'as an unfriendly act',[2] the other considered that the 'Soviet—Pakistan arms deal is a slap in India's face, though Mr Kosygin and Moscovite patriots would like us to believe that it is the fond caress of an abiding friend'.[3] A number of national and regional papers went to the extent of arguing in favour of normalizing relations with China in order to counter Soviet action. 'India', suggested *Pioneer*, 'must open a new window to escape from the present oppressive and stultifying atmosphere or face the certainty of an ignominious surrender either to Russia or to the United States as the price of protection which may even involve signing away her rights to Pakistan.'[4]

The attitude of the Indian Government was, however, cautious. After having made a number of discreet and vain efforts to dissuade Moscow from taking such a decision, some members of the Central Government, according to different reports, manifested their irritation by leaking the news to the Indian press. It was calculated that 'a popular outburst' that would inevitably result from such a leakage would not be a bad idea and might actually persuade the Soviet leaders to renege from their original decision.[5] At about the same time, the Indian Prime Minister, Mrs Gandhi, publicly reacted by stating that 'we are not happy' about the Soviet decision, though she prudently made it clear that Indian foreign policy would not undergo 'any change'.[6] The Defence Minister went a little further and expressed the view that the Soviet Union and the United States were making 'a wrong assessment' by supplying arms to Pakistan, thus encouraging her to adopt a 'more intransigent attitude' towards India.[7]

The official circumspection can by no means be attributed—as has been suggested by some Indian circles—to the pro-Soviet proclivities of the Indian decision-makers; for hardly any one of them was either attracted or influenced by the paradigm of Soviet thinking. On the contrary, the Soviet economic and political system did not inspire any meaningful confidence among many of them.

[1] *People's Democracy* (14 July 1968).

[2] From the *Hindu*, cited by 'Nireekshak', 'What then must we do', *Economic and Political Weekly* (27 August 1968).

[3] From *Indian Express*, cited in *ibid*.   [4] *Ibid*.   [5] *Ibid*.

[6] *The Statesman's Weekly* (13 July 1968).   [7] *Ibid*. (23 November 1968).

The Indian prudence was dictated by a number of very practical reasons to which sufficient importance has not been given. In the first place, it was simply not possible for the Indian Government to rock the boat of Indo-Soviet relations at a time when India was heavily dependent on the Soviet Union on a number of issues of foreign policy; for the dangerous consequences that would have resulted from such an action would have, in all probability, outweighed the advantages—if any—that India would have gained from such a policy. Secondly, the government of India had been repeatedly assured by Moscow that whatever arms the Soviet Union might supply to Pakistan would pose no danger to India.[1] On the contrary, argued the Soviets, with arms supplies, Soviet influence over Pakistan should increase and this influence would undoubtedly be exercised against military adventures. Thirdly, most of the sophisticated military hardware that India received from the outside emanated from the Soviet Union; and most of the financial and technical assistance also came from that country.[2]

In view of all this, what could India do and from whom could she obtain military hardware, if she defied Moscow? Military aid from the United States and Great Britain was no longer possible in view of their decision to stop all such assistance in the aftermath of the Indo-Pakistan war of 1965. Nor was it possible—at least at the moment—for her to normalize her relations with Pakistan and China, for conflicts with both of them were too aggravated and too forlorn to be resolved easily.

India, thus, was left with no options, and had apparently no choice but to continue to maintain relations with Moscow, notwithstanding the difficulties that had bubbled to the surface as a result of the Soviet armed assistance to Pakistan.

(b) Difficulties in Indo-Soviet relations

However, notwithstanding the limited options, the relations between the two countries did not radiate the same warmth and the same level of friendliness as existed in the mid-fifties. They were in fact seriously affected. The level of frankness and cordiality that had existed before had become strikingly low; and the Soviet and Indian statements made in private meetings now were simple reiterations of what had been publicly

[1] Kosygin made a statement to this effect in Calcutta on 10 September 1964. See *The Statesman's Weekly* (13 September 1969).

[2] For details see *supra*, pp. 53–65.

stated. The Soviet attitude, for example, at the Indo-Soviet bilateral talks held in Delhi in 1968, was that of an imperial power dealing with a dependency. She did not even observe the elementary diplomatic courtesies, as they brushed aside one Indian query after another, and studiously refused to offer satisfaction to the host country on any matter of direct concern to her. Whether the issue was the supply of Soviet arms to Pakistan or Moscow's neutralist stand on Kashmir or the continuous propaganda against Indian leaders that was regularly beamed by Soviet *Radio Peace and Progress*. Even on the question of border alignment between India and China, shown on Soviet maps, the attitude of the Soviet delegation was generally evasive and non-committal.[1]

But the differences between the two countries are no more confined to a few political issues only. They have spilled over to the economic domain, where increasing number of difficulties and differences have become evident on the question of trade relations, on the issues of projects financed by the Soviet Union, on the further development of the oil industry, etc.

On the question of trade, difficulties began to arise with the development of a favourable trade balance for India. This began in 1964 and reached the figure of 210 million rupees in 1967.[2] Such a trend is expected to continue in view of the fact that, having built an important industrial base, Indian needs for capital equipment have significantly declined, and her demand for such commodities as fertilizers, newsprint, industrial raw materials, non-ferrous metals, etc., are rapidly rising.[3] The Soviet Union, which had so far met most of India's demands for capital equipment, is however unable to provide the new needs.

But she appears none the less to be insisting that India must buy from her in order to balance the trade and payments between the two countries. The controversy over Soviet aircraft is an example of some of the difficulties that have begun to bubble to the surface between New Delhi and Moscow. Moscow has been making special efforts to persuade the Indians to buy TU-134 for their domestic air services. Such an agreement, point out the Russians, would be advantageous to India in view of the fact that

[1] For some details about the bilateral talks, see 'Chorus', 'A chill contact between India and Russia', *The Statesman* (24 September 1968). See also Kuldip Nayar, *op. cit.*, p. 99.

[2] *Financial Times* (12 June 1968).

[3] Indian imports of industrial raw materials between April–September 1968 were 40 per cent higher compared to the same period during 1967. *Statesman* (9 February 1969).

she can pay in rupees. Further, this would make it possible to re-establish a balance of trade and payments between the two countries.

The Indians, however, have some difficulties in accepting the Soviet offer, in view of the fact that the Soviet aircraft involves high operating and maintenance costs. Apparently the Soviet airlines have not been concerned much with cost accounting. While these considerations have not been very important for Soviet and East European operators, they are of primordial importance to commercial airlines in other countries, whether or not they are state owned.

Consequently, the Indian Government has declined to accept the Soviet offer,[1] and finally opted for one of the western planes.[2] But the authorities in New Delhi had displayed considerable hesitation and uncertainty in taking a decision to this effect, despite the recommendation of the expert body appointed to study the question. The political consequences of such a decision were obviously very important and they had to be taken into account before a final decision could be taken, particularly when Moscow, according to some reports, had begun to show signs of delaying the conclusion of an important agreement to buy 54,000 railway wagons from India.[3]

Difficulties also began to arise in some of the projects built by Moscow. Some of them were ill-equipped, while the others were in fields for which there did not appear to be much demand. For instance, The Indian Drugs and Pharmaceuticals Ltd (IDPL) was dogged from the outset by faulty equipment, rising costs, designs unsuitable for Indian conditions, and delays in delivery. It was even suggested that much of the plant was in fact second-hand, having been built for China and dismantled. The Soviet project report had not included a feasibility study, estimates of demand having been assumed from Soviet experience elsewhere. Consequently, there was a heavy surplus at the plant. Indian consumption of the tetracycline group of drugs, for instance, was ten metric tons a year and was estimated to rise to 40–50 metric tons by 1971–72. But the Soviet experts none the less insisted on a capacity of 120 tons of chlorotetracycline which had become obsolete and was not used by Indian doctors. The IDPL consequently incurred a loss of 8·9 million rupees in 1968.[4]

The Indian Parliamentary Committee on Public Undertakings in April 1969 accused Soviet experts of 'tremendous underestimation of production costs'. Vitamin B^1 was estimated at 100 rupees per kg, while the actual

[1] *The Statesman's Weekly* (7 December 1968).   [2] *Ibid.* (8 February 1968).
[3] *Indian Express* (11 August 1969).
[4] *Economic and Political Weekly* (5 October 1968).

cost finally worked out was 1,200 rupees per kg. The Russians had insisted too that the plant should produce penicillin, although sufficient quantities for Indian needs were already being produced elsewhere in the country. It was found that the surgical instruments plant was not economic unless it worked at full capacity, but the demand was much lower because between 60–73 per cent of the Soviet specified instruments were not acceptable to Indian surgeons. The IDPL chairman stated on 14 December 1968 that they were 'too big for Indian hands'. But the Russians insisted that unwanted instruments be produced and in one case as many as 19,666 instruments of a particular type were produced in 1966–67, although only one had been sold the previous year.[1]

One could venture to suggest that at present the capacity of most of the Soviet-aided plants—ranging from the mammoth steel mill at Bhilai to the heavy engineering corporation at Ranchi—are working below capacity because of the lack of demand for their products. Bhilai's production, for example, at 1·76 million tons in 1966, was at the rate of utilization less than 100 per cent as against 109 to 113 per cent in 1964. Stocks have continued to accumulate. The pig-iron stocks on 1 March 1967 amounted to 83,000 tons against 45,000 tons in 1966, and those of rolled steel aggregated to 171,000 tons against 55,000 tons in 1966.[2]

Moscow is consequently reported to have informed New Delhi, during Staklov's visit in January 1969, that no further Soviet assistance would be forthcoming unless 28 existing projects were made to run economically. In fact, according to a report, he was far from flattering about the performance of the Russian-aided projects and expressed himself 'in language which far exceeded the bounds of frankness expected from a friend and came very close to rudeness'.[3]

With regard to those industries that were working below capacity, the Soviet Government had placed large orders for steel, rail and wagon plants to enable these plants to work at full capacity, since they have been planned to operate economically only when operating at peak production. But recently, however, there has developed an increasing reluctance to place orders, and greater efforts are being made to impress upon India to find markets for their products elsewhere and not depend on Moscow to buy surplus products.[4] The Soviet Government is reported, however, to

[1] *Current* (14 December 1968).   [2] *Eastern Economist* (29 December 1967), p. 1200.
[3] Inder Malhotra, 'Wrong Men in Top Jobs. The Bane of the Public Sector', *The Statesman's Weekly* (25 January 1969).
[4] *Financial Times* (5 December 1968).

have promised to assist India in finding markets in third countries for complete plants manufactured under Soviet-aided projects.[1]

Difficulties are also discernible in the further development of the oil industry. After having acquired a dominant position in the Indian oil industry, the Soviet Union is eager not to lose this position. The Soviet attitude to the exploring of oil in structures discovered off the Bombay coastline in the gulf of Cambay is a case in point.[2] Preliminary investigations in 1963 indicated that these structures held promise of being some of the largest oil reserves in the world. It is interesting that Moscow admitted that its own expertise was inadequate to explore and develop the structures. But, at the same time, it would not have other countries undertake the work, and has been pressurizing the Indian Government to go slow in the hope that it will be able to satisfy Indian technical needs within a few years. In fact, the Soviet Government is reported to have exercised considerable pressure on Mrs Gandhi not to endorse a draft agreement that was concluded by the Ministry of Petroleum and Chemicals with Tennco, the United States oil company.[3]

The factor that perhaps contributed to the rise of most serious differences in Indo-Soviet relations was the whole issue of the quantum of Indian participation in the implementation of Soviet-aided projects. The Soviet Union had been used to the idea of bearing complete responsibility for the designing and the planning of the physical outlay of the project. The Bhilai steel plant had been constructed completely by the Soviet Union. However, with the increasing sophistication of the Indian industrial development and the rapid increase in India's technical manpower, her needs of outside technical assistance for the implementation of the projects have significantly diminished. Therefore the Indian Government, in response to the new development, tends increasingly to question some of the plans submitted by the Russian experts, and has proposed changes in the designing and the financial outlay of the projects. This has often led to the development of some friction between the two governments. The negotiations on the Bokaro project is a case in point. The Soviet Government declined to share the construction of the project with Indian consultants and forced on India 350 Soviet experts when the Indian Government was convinced that Indian engineers could do the job.[4] This

---

[1] *Times of India* (20 December 1968).

[2] *Thought* (14 September 1968). See also *Economic and Political Weekly* (7 September 1968).

[3] *Ibid.*   [4] *The Statesman's Weekly* (14 May 1966).

was described by an observer as 'an attempt to reduce us to that of contractor-coolies'.[1] The Indian proposal of an economy of 20 billion rupees in a project of 90 billion was also rejected. Moscow very clearly told New Delhi that either it could approve the project along with the original costs of production or alternatively drop it altogether. Further-more, there have been four delays since the project was conceived in 1964 which have put the estimated completion date of the first stage to early 1973 compared with the original schedule of late 1968. These delays have pushed up the cost of the project over and over again to a fantastic figure. The Soviet consultants had originally undertaken to complete the first stage of the project at a cost of 5 billion and 900 million rupees. It is now likely to be around 8 billion rupees.[2]

A further point of controversy surrounding the Bokaro project is the decision to import refractories (heat-resisting materials) for the coke ovens from the Soviet Union rather than using locally produced models, even though two refractory units situated near Bokaro had to be closed down due to lack of orders. While the Bokaro plant authorities blame the local manufacturers for delays in deliveries, the manufacturers have repeatedly complained that the specifications laid down by Russian planners 'have been needlessly rigid and stringent'.[3] Although a committee was set up to investigate the dispute, the Soviet experts made it clear that no change in the specification would be accepted.

In addition to all these difficulties, the over-all Soviet attitude towards India became more and more difficult. More and more examples began to arise of Soviet annoyance with India, difficulties began to surge forward regarding the composition of delegations, criticism of internal Indian policies became more rampant in the Soviet press and anti-Indian propaganda—including personal attacks on right-wing leaders—became increasingly common on *Radio Peace and Progress*. Particularly during the general elections in 1967, the broadcasts openly supported the oppo-nents of the Congress party. The Communist-dominated governments, which were returned to power in Kerala and West Bengal, were subse-quently welcomed, with continued stress on the danger of 'right-wing reaction'. In May 1967, the building of a 'united left front' was put forward as 'the duty of every patriot, of every democratic party', while the Communists were described as 'the genuine defenders of the interests of the working people'. When the Indian Government protested to the Soviet Government for interfering in the internal affairs of India, the

[1] *Economic Times* (17 October 1964).   [2] *Ibid.* (4 February 1970).
[3] *The Hindu* (30 January 1970).

Soviet Government simply rejected Indian protest on the ground that critical broadcasts emanating from *Radio Peace and Progress* were by a private and independent organization and not an official concern.[1]

Soviet ideological assessment of the Indian political and economic scene also underwent an important change by the middle sixties. That is to say that it became increasingly critical of India and her leadership. Since Nehru's death, in the Soviet view, there has been a growing 'polarization of class forces', and an increasing deviation from original internal and external policies.

The *New Times* noted India's increasing dependence on United States aid and the 'growing strength of the capitalist monopolies with their close foreign ties'.[2] While praising the projects and developments employing Soviet aid, a continuous stress was laid on the numerous indications of shortcomings by the ruling Congress party: its 'inconsistent and hesitant' approach to agrarian problems opening the way to an 'onslaught of the right'; its recourse to foreign (i.e. American) aid in food emergencies; and its record, as instanced by the list of disturbances, of 'arousing popular discontent and sharpening social conflict'.[3] After the general elections, Mrs Indira Gandhi's cabinet was considered 'as a coalition of the ruling party's centrist and rightist elements'.[4] In still another study, undertaken by Professor R. Ulyanovsky, deputy head of the International Department of the Soviet Central Committee, India along with Pakistan was rated below the more recently independent countries in Africa in terms of revolutionary potential. The functioning of the state sector in India was considered to be far from promising in view of the fact that it was being 'gradually converted into a means of speeding up the development of privately-owned industrial capitalism'. The effect of this and other 'retrograde' tendencies was, according to Ulanovsky, to cancel out such favourable Indian features as 'a progressive foreign policy' and 'friendly relations with the Soviet camp'.[5] Perhaps the most penetrating analysis of the socio-economic alignments in India appeared in an article in *International Affairs*. The author, M. Savelyev, noticed a radical shift within the system of Indian big business, and in the Indian monopolies who had severely extended their control over vital sectors of Indian economy, and who in co-operation with western monopoly capital were putting pressure on the government to abandon its progressive policies.[6]

He particularly noted:

[1] *The Times* (18 March 1970).   [2] *New Times* (11 August 1965).
[3] *Ibid.* (16 August 1967).   [4] *Ibid.*   [5] *Pravda* (3 January 1968).
[6] *International Affairs* (April 1967).

As the tide of reaction mounted, social antagonisms were intensified and sharpened between labour and capital, small landless peasants and big landowners, democracy and monopoly, and the demands for the country's economic independence and the neo-colonialist schemes of imperialism. Government attempts to undo the tight knot of contradictions proved to be generally ineffective. The big monopoly and imperialist circles, taking advantage of the government's vacillation and playing up the economic and foreign policy criticism, were deliberately stirring up internal political tensions with a view to stifling democracy, depriving the working class of its social and class gains and pushing India off the path of independence.[1]

However, all the difficulties that have surged forward between the two countries do not seem to interfere with Soviet efforts to forge closer links with India. Apparently, the geo-political and national interest considerations tend to be goading the Soviet leadership to continue to take positive steps to cultivate Indian friendship. India still remains an important factor in international affairs; for notwithstanding the considerable plummeting of her prestige after 1962, her large size, her relative political stability and reasonable economic growth cannot be ignored by any power—least of all by the Soviet Union who is continuously seeking a viable counter-balance to the expanding Chinese influence on the continent of Asia.

[1] *International Affairs* (April 1967).

CONCLUSIONS

Between the two world wars, Europe occupied a prime place in Soviet diplomacy. It was towards this continent that the Bolshevik leaders first of all turned in order to incite Communist revolutions. And it was in this part of the world that they primarily concentrated their offensive and defensive diplomatic actions once it became apparent that revolutions had failed. In fact, so overwhelmingly important was this factor in Soviet operational diplomacy that one cannot escape the reflection that Moscow's policy towards Asia was often influenced by its requirements in Europe. A hardening of Soviet policy in Europe, for example, invariably led to the embarkation of revolutionary offensives in Asia, and a shift to a policy of moderation on that continent very often culminated in the implementation of soft policy in the area.

This subordination of Asia to Europe was dictated by a number of concrete and objective factors. In the first place, the first Communist revolution had been successful in relatively under-developed Russia, when according to all Marxist prognostications it should have sparked in the industrially developed countries, where despite the existence of appropriate conditions for continuous economic development, the modern labourer continued to sink 'deeper and deeper below the conditions of existence of his own class'.[1]

Such an unexpected development—obviously due to a fortuitous combination of circumstances—was bound to create, in the Marxist view, serious difficulties in the successful attainment of socialism in Russia, unless of course a Communist revolution could be successfully staged in an advanced European country which could assist her in reaching the economic level that was considered as an indispensable condition for the success of socialism. Therefore, during the first few years after the Bolshevik revolution, the Soviet leaders were preoccupied with the task of manœuvring Communist revolutions in Europe; even when it became apparent by the middle twenties that the original hope of revolutions in Europe had vanished, consequently resulting in the adoption of the Stalinist concept of 'socialism in one country', a general conviction none

[1] Karl Marx and Frederick Engels, 'Manifesto of the Communist Party', *Selected Works*, Vol. 1 (Moscow: 1946), p. 121.

the less prevailed among the Soviet leaders that the successful completion of a socialist society in Soviet Russia was hardly attainable, considering the difficult task of economic development that faced the country. The Asian countries, still far removed from the goal of political independence and economic development, could scarcely fulfil such an important function. In fact, one could venture to suggest that Communist revolutions in these countries would have hindered the economic development of Soviet Russia for she would have felt obliged in this case, for the sake of international solidarity, to come to their assistance, thereby diverting what appeared to be limited Soviet resources.

Secondly, the Soviet leaders did not look to Europe only with expectancy and hope. They also dreaded the undermining of their own revolution through attacks originating from that continent. Such a fear was perhaps not unfounded, for some responsible European leaders had publicly manifested their displeasure at the developments in Russia; and many more had announced their intention to destroy the revolutionary government before it acquired all the characteristics of a stable régime.

Thirdly, during the inter-war years, Soviet Russia, despite her geographical position both as a European and an Asian country, was still a regional power who did not possess the sinews of military and political power to undertake effective actions in areas which happened to be distant from the heart of Russia. And the heart of Russia for the Bolsheviks, during the inter-war period, was situated in Europe, for it was in this area that there existed the core of Russia's industrial and military complex.

Fourthly, the Soviet Government and the Comintern were dominated by Europeans who never succeeded in ridding themselves of a European bias and who felt that their obligations towards Asia were satisfied with the occasional adoption of theoretical formulations. At the second congress of the Comintern, where Lenin's national and colonial thesis figured prominently, most of the delegates displayed a lack of any genuine interest on the question and appeared to be eager to pass on to the other items on the agenda.[1] For them, revolutions in Germany and France were more real than upheavals in India and Indonesia. Even Lenin, who had projected Asia on the European-oriented Comintern congresses, was hesitant in assigning a predominant role to Asia. While accepting the revolutionary potentialities of Asia he, however, continued to maintain the original Marxist view that socialism was possible in countries which were industrially advanced.

[1] M. N. Roy, *op. cit.*, p. 384.

Immediately after World War II, Europe continued to hold the attention of the Soviet leaders, for it was there that the aftermath of war had brought economic dislocation, political instability, and the consequent hope of revolutionary upheavals. Almost half of Europe had come under Soviet control, and the Communist parties in France and Italy had been catapulted into positions of considerable power in the political lives of their countries.

It was thus inevitable that the development of such a situation would only reinforce Soviet revolutionary mood, and encourage them to view with great expectancy the future prospects of Communism in Europe. Concomitantly, one also began to witness the return of Soviet leadership to those attitudes of suspicion and hostility towards the West, which it had repeatedly expressed before World War II.

Was this feeling of belligerence a natural consequence of the revolutionary mood that was rampant among the Soviet leaders, or was it a reaction to the action of the western powers? It is of course difficult to say with any certainty. One thing is, however, certain: the combination of all these factors, together with the rapid degeneration of the over-all political situation, generated an atmosphere of unparalleled hostility in Europe. On a number of occasions the spiral of explosive actions and reactions produced the uneasy feeling that Europe was sitting on a barrel of gunpowder. What was perhaps even worse was the widespread fear that this was not a meteoric crisis which would disappear in time, but something which Europeans would have to live with indefinitely. In any case, the development of such a situation generated new hopes of kindling revolutionary fires in the heart of Europe.

However, within two or three years after the war, the Soviet hope of exercising significant influence in Western Europe was dispelled. Despite the existence of mass Communist parties in France and Italy, Western Europe, with United States assistance, rapidly asserted its determination to become stable and to remain non-Communist. It was no longer possible for the Soviet Union to make any further diplomatic headway in Europe, to increase her political influence or break up some of the intractable deadlocks that haunted the Continent. This situation has not changed. Despite the disengagement of France from the United States, despite the remarkable demolition of economic and cultural barriers that one is now witnessing between the two blocs, the Continent still remains profoundly partitioned politically and militarily, with no scope for Moscow to advance its political cause on the other side of the barrier. If anything, it is the Soviet political and ideological influence that appears to be on the decline in Eastern Europe.

The situation in Asia, by contrast, was far from stable. The political lines were not sharply drawn and, unlike Western Europe, the Asian countries did not have any reason to consider that they had nothing to learn from the Soviet socialist experiment. Furthermore, as a result of the stresses and strains engendered by World War II, almost all the countries of the region were undergoing profound revolutionary changes. The decolonization process, to which the Soviet leaders had been giving their continuous support since the revolution, had set in, bringing independence to some countries and assuring it to the others. Even more significant for Moscow were the events in China where the Communist Party, relying principally on its own strength, had finally consummated its revolution in 1949 after years of harsh and bitter struggle.

The Soviet Union, which had already attained the status of a super-power, could hardly ignore these developments. It could hardly permit its objectives in Europe to continue to determine its policy in Asia. To do so would have meant, in effect, the abdication of hegemony to the Communist Party of China, which had already moved to arrogate to itself the leadership of the Asian revolutionary world, and which had demonstrated its bent towards independent thinking, much to Moscow's displeasure. With the rapidity that is often strikingly remarkable in Soviet response to new situations, one began to witness, after the late forties, a growing Soviet involvement in the whirlpool of Asian politics. The quantum of official declarations, articles and diplomatic initiatives that pertained to Asia was indeed considerable. And today, it is evident that the continent of Asia, along with the rest of the third world, has come to occupy a central place in Soviet diplomacy.

Within the framework of Soviet policy in Asia, India undoubtedly has come to occupy a very significant place in Soviet operational diplomacy. In fact, one could even venture to suggest that during the decade following the death of Stalin, she had acquired a position of centrality. The economic and military aid that was given, the political support that was extended, and the spate of Soviet literature published on India is an important proof of this policy. Such a political line is understandable; for India—in addition to her big size and strategic location—was politically stable and industrially more developed than the other countries of the region. Furthermore, the policy of non-alignment, so sedulously developed by Nehru, had given her a unique moral stature among the Afro-Asian countries. A close co-operation with India, it was probably felt, would

H

make it relatively easier for the Soviet Union to vitiate and forestall the influence of unfriendly powers in the area.

The rise of Soviet interest in India, therefore, was not only due to her inherent importance, but also to her potential power and ability to skew the delicate Asian balance in Soviet favour. It was the United States' policy of containment which, to a large measure, emboldened the Soviet Union to seek India's friendship in 1954. And it was the exacerbation of the Sino-Soviet dispute which led the Soviet leaders in 1960 increasingly to turn towards New Delhi in order to counter the expanding Chinese influence.

After the fall of Khruschev in 1964, a subtle permutation became discernible in Soviet policy. India was no longer the focal point of Soviet diplomacy in Asia. Some of the other nations of the continent, having successfully manifested a measure of assertiveness in international affairs, also increasingly became objects of Soviet attention.

A number of reasons can be attributed to the generation of this change, but the most important were two: in the first place, there appears to have developed latterly a general trend in Soviet policy to extricate itself from an immoderate involvement in intractable problems that are of no direct concern to vital Soviet interests. And the Indo-Pakistan conflict, though important because of the Sino-Soviet dispute, does not directly affect Soviet interests.

The adoption of such a political line is not only a striking example of growing sophistication in Soviet diplomatic behaviour, but is perhaps an important sign of general Soviet consensus that this, under the circumstances, is the only effective way to safeguard Soviet national interest, and at the same time aggrandize Soviet influence.

Secondly, India by the early sixties had ceased to carry great weight in international affairs. Since the Sino-Indian War of 1962 it had become increasingly evident that she did not have the necessary political and military strength to defend her interests and her security. For the Soviet Union, which was obviously seeking an effective counter-balance to the rising Chinese influence in the area, the Indian performance must have been a source of great disappointment, and was probably instrumental in encouraging her to jettison her rather very special relations with India.

None the less, despite the considerable plummeting of her world image since 1962, India still remains an important factor in international relations. Her size is too large, her population too big, her strategic location too important to be ignored by any major power which has firm intentions of playing a vital role in Asia. It is therefore most unlikely that she would become a marginal factor in Soviet policy towards Asia, though it is also unlikely that she would ever re-acquire the same important position as she had during the Khruschev period.

SELECT BIBLIOGRAPHY

I. SOURCES

1. Official and Unofficial Publications

INDIA

Lok Sabha Secretariat, *Foreign Policy of India. Texts of Documents*. New Delhi: 1958.

Ministry of Commerce, *India's Trade Agreements*. New Delhi: 1968.

Ministry of External Affairs, *Prime Minister on Sino-Indian Relations*. 2 Vols. New Delhi: 1962.

Ministry of External Affairs, *Notes, Memoranda, Letters and Agreements Signed between the Governments of India and China*. 1954–62. 6 Vols. New Delhi: 1962.

Ministry of Information and Broadcasting, *Jawaharlal Nehru's Speeches*. 1946–49; 1949–53; and 1953–57. New Delhi: 1953, 1954, 1958.

——, *Speeches of Prime Minister Lal Bahadur Shastri*. New Delhi: 1965.

SOVIET UNION

Chernenko, K. U. (ed.) *et al.*, *Soviet Foreign Policy. Basic Acts and Documents of the Supreme Soviet of the USSR*. Moscow: Foreign Languages Publishing House, 1962.

Eudin, X. J., and North, Robert C., *Soviet Russia and the East, 1920–1927. A Documentary Survey*. Stanford: Stanford University Press, 1957.

Khruschev, N. S., *Soviet Union: Faithful Friend of the Peoples of the East. N. S. Khruschev's Speeches made during his Visit to India, Burma, Indonesia and Afghanistan*. New Delhi: Soviet Land Booklets, 1960.

——, *World Without Arms, World Without Wars*. 2 Vols. Moscow: Foreign Languages Publishing House, n.d.

——, *Communism—Peace and Happiness for the Peoples*. Moscow: Foreign Languages Press, 1963.

——, *Prevent War, Safeguard Peace*. Moscow: Progress Publishers, 1963.

Lenin, V. I., *The National-Liberation Movement in the East*. Moscow: Foreign Languages Publishing House, 1957.

——, *On the Foreign Policy of the Soviet State*. Moscow: Progress Publishers, n.d.

2. Other Sources

Chinese People's Institute of Foreign Affairs, *The Sino-Indian Boundary Question*. Peking: Foreign Languages Press, 1960.

Hasan, Sarwar K. (ed.), *Documents on the Foreign Relations of Pakistan. China India Pakistan*. Karachi: Pakistan Institute of International Affairs, 1966.

3. Memoirs, Autobiographies and Journals

Ayub Khan, Mohammad, *Friends Not Masters. A Political Autobiography*. London: Oxford University Press, 1967.

Bowles, Chester, *Ambassador's Report*. New York: Harper & Brothers, 1954.

Galbraith, John Kenneth, *Ambassador's Journal. A Personal Account of the Kennedy Years*. London: Hamish Hamilton, 1969.

Menon, K. P. S., *The Flying Troika. Extracts from a Diary*. London: Oxford University Press, 1963.

Nehru, Jawaharlal, *Towards Freedom: The Autobiography of Jawaharlal Nehru*. New York: John Day, 1942.

Pannikar, K. M., *In Two Chinas. Memoirs of a Diplomat*. London: Allen & Unwin, 1955.

Roy, M. N., *M. N. Roy's Memoirs*. Bombay: Allied Publishers Private Ltd, 1964.

4. Newspapers and Periodicals

International Affairs (Moscow).
Izvestia (Moscow).
New Times (Moscow).
People's China (Peking).
Peking Review (Peking).
Pravda (Moscow).
Soviet News (London).

II. STUDIES

1. Books

Balabushevich, V. V., and Prasad, Bimla (ed.), *India and the Soviet Union*. New Delhi: People's Publishing House, 1969.

Brecher, Michael, *Nehru. A Political Biography*. London: Oxford University Press, 1959.

Brines, Russell, *The Indo-Pakistani Conflict*. London: Pall Mall Press, 1968.

Brown, Norman W., *The United States and India and Pakistan*. 2nd ed. Cambridge: Harvard Univerity Press, 1963.

Chakravarti, P. C., *India's China Policy*. Bloomington, Ind.: Indiana University Press, 1962.

Chopra, Pran, *Uncertain India. A Political Profile of Two Decades of Freedom*. Bombay: Asia Publishing House, 1968.

Choudhury, G. W., *Pakistan's Relations with India. 1947–1966*. London: Pall Mall Press, 1969.

Clarkson, Stephen, *L'analyse soviétique des problèmes indiens du sous-developpement*. Paris: 1965. Ph.D. dissertation.

Diakov, A. M., *New Stage in India's Liberation Struggle*. Bombay: People's Publishing House, 1950.

Druhe, David N., *Soviet Russia and Indian Communism*. New York: Bookman Associates, 1959.

Gupta, Bhabani Sen, *The Fulcrum of Asia. Relations among China, India, Pakistan and the USSR*. New York: Pegasus, 1970.

Gupta, Hari Ram, *India-Pakistan War 1965*. 2 Vols. Delhi: Hariyana Prakashan, 1968.

Gupta, Anand (ed.), *India and Lenin. A Collection*. New Delhi: New Literature, 1960.

Harrison, Selig G., *India. The Most Dangerous Decades*. Madras: Oxford University Press, 1960.

Imam, Zafar, *Colonialism in East-West Relations. A Study of Soviet Policy towards India and Anglo-Soviet Relations 1917–1947*. New Delhi: Eastman Publications, 1969.

Indian Institute of Foreign Trade, *India's Trade with Eastern Europe*. New Delhi: Directorate of Commercial Publicity, Ministry of Commerce, 1966.

Jansen, G. H., *Nonalignment and the Afro-Asian States*. New York: Frederick A. Praeger, 1966.

Johnson, William A., *The Steel Industry of India*. Cambridge, Mass.: Harvard University Press, 1955.

Kapur, Harish, *Soviet Russia and Asia, 1917–1927. A Study of Soviet Policy towards Turkey, Iran and Afghanistan*. London: Michael Joseph, 1966.

Karanjia, R. K., *The Mind of Nehru. An Interview*. London: George Allen and Unwin Ltd, 1960.

——, *The Philosophy of Mr. Nehru. As Revealed in a Series of Intimate Talks with R. K. Karanjia*. London: George Allen and Unwin Ltd, 1966.

Karunakaran, K. P. (ed.), *Outside the Conflict. A Study of Non-alignment and the Foreign Policy of some of the Non-aligned Countries*. New Delhi: People's Publishing House, 1963.

——, *India in World Affairs 1950–1953*. Calcutta: Oxford University Press, 1958.

Kautsky, John H., *Moscow and the Communist Party of India: A Study in the Postwar Evolution of International Communist Strategy*. New York: Wiley and Sons, 1956.

Kavic, Lorne J., *India's Quest for Security 1947–65*. Berkeley: University of California Press, 1967.

Kulkarni, Maya, *Indo-Soviet Political Relations*. Bombay: Vora and Co., 1968.

Kundra, J. C., *Indian Foreign Policy 1947–54. A Study of Relations with Western Bloc*. Bombay: Vora, 1955.

Levi, W., *Free India in Asia*. Minneapolis: University of Minnesota Press, 1954.

Masani, M. R., *The Communist Party of India. A Short History*. London: Derek Verschoyle, 1954.

McLane, Charles B., *Soviet Strategies in South East Asia. An Exploration of Eastern Policy under Lenin and Stalin*. Princeton: Princeton University Press, 1966.

Melman, Sofia, *Foreign Monopoly Capital in Indian Economy*. New Delhi: People's Publishing House, 1963.

Miller, J. D. B. (ed.), *India, Japan, Australia Partners in Asia?* Canberra: Australian National University Press, 1968.

Moraes, Frank, *Jawaharlal Nehru. A Biography*. Bombay: Jaico Publishing House, 1959.

Naik, J. A., *Soviet Policy towards India. From Stalin to Brezhnev*. Delhi: Vikas Publications, 1970.

Nayar, Kuldip, *Between the Lines*. New Delhi: Allied Publishers Private Ltd, 1969.

Nehru, Jawaharlal, *Soviet Russia: Some Random Sketches and Impressions.* Bombay: Chetana, 1960.

——, *The Discovery of India.* London: Meridian Books Ltd, 1960.

——, *India Today and Tomorrow.* New Delhi: Orient Longmans Private Ltd, 1960.

Overstreet, Gene D., and Windmiller, Marshall, *Communism in India.* Berkeley: University of California Press, 1959.

Pannikar, K. M., *Problems of Indian Defence.* New York: Asia Publishing House, 1960.

——, *India and the Indian Ocean.* London: George Allen and Unwin Ltd, 1951.

——, *Geographical Factors in Indian History.* Bombay: Bharatiya Vidya Bhavan, 1955.

Ranadive, B. T., *The Crisis of Indian Economy.* Bombay: People's Publishing House Ltd, 1954.

Rymalov, V., *La collaboration économique de l'URSS avec les pays sous-développés.* Moscow: Foreign Languages Press, n.d.

Sager, Peter, *Moscow's Hand in India.* Berne: Swiss Eastern Institute, 1966.

Samra, Chattar Singh, *India and Anglo-Soviet Relations 1917–1947.* Bombay: Asia Publishing House, 1959.

Sardesai, S. G., *India and the Russian Revolution.* New Delhi: New Age Printing Press, 1967.

Sawyer, Carole A., *Communist Trade with Developing Countries 1955–65.* New York: Praeger, 1966.

Sen, Bhowani, *Evolution of Agrarian Relations in India.* New Delhi: People's Publishing House, 1962.

Sherwani, Laty Ahmed *et al.*, *Foreign Policy of Pakistan. An Analysis.* Karachi: The Allies Book Corporation, 1964.

Stein, Arthur, *India and the Soviet Union. The Nehru Era.* Chicago: The Chicago University Press, 1969.

Talbot, Phillips, *India and America. A Study of their Relations.* New York: Harper & Brothers, 1958.

Tanzer, Michael, *The Political Economy of International Oil and the Under-developed Countries.* London: Temple Smith, 1969.

Thien, Ton That, *India and South East Asia 1947–1960. A Study of India's Policy towards the South East Asian Countries in the Period 1947–60.* Geneva: Librairie Droz, 1963.

Thornton, Thomas Perry (intr.), *The Third World in Soviet Perspective:*

Studies by Soviet Writers on the Developing Areas. Princeton: Princeton University Press, 1964.

Wint, Guy (ed.), *Asia Handbook*. London: Penguin Books, 1969.

2. Selected Articles

Ballis, William B., 'Recent Soviet Relations with India', *Studies in the Soviet Union*, No. 1, 1963.

Chaudhri, M. A., 'Pakistan's Relations with the Soviet Union', *Asian Survey*, September 1966.

Demaitre, E., 'Soviet-Indian Relations, Neutralism and Communist China', *Russian Review*, No. 22, 1963.

Gopal, S., 'India, China and the Soviet Union', *Australian Journal of Politics and History*, August 1966.

Graham, Ian, 'The Indo-Soviet MIG Deal and its International Repercussions', *Asian Survey*, May 1964.

Gupta, Bhabani Sen, 'Moscow, Peking and the Indian Political Scene after Nehru', *Orbis*, Summer 1968.

Gupta, K., 'A Study of Indo-Soviet Relations 1946–1955', *Calcutta Review*, April 1956.

Gupta, Karunakaran, 'Indo-Soviet Relations in Retrospect', *Afro-Asian and World Affairs*, Autumn 1965.

Kapur, Harish, 'USSR and Indo-Pakistan Relations', *International Studies*, July–October 1966.

Morris, G. B., 'India and Pakistan, 1953–1960. The Soviet Version', *Soviet Survey*, July–September 1960.

Nair, K., 'Where India, China and Russia Meet', *Foreign Affairs*, January 1958.

Savelyev, N., 'Monopoly Drive in India', *International Affairs*, No. 4, 1967.

Simon, Sheldon W., 'The Kashmir Dispute in Sino-Soviet Perspective', *Asian Survey*, March 1967.

Stein, Arthur, 'India's Relations with the USSR, 1953–1963', *Journal of Politics*, February 1963.

Vaidyanath, R., 'Some Trends in Soviet Policies towards India and Pakistan', *International Studies*, January 1966.

Yudin, P., 'Can We Accept Pandit Nehru's Approach?', *World Marxist Review*, December 1958.

Zubeida, Hasan, 'Soviet Arms Aid to Pakistan and India', *Pakistan Horizon*, No. 4, 1969.

3. Newspapers and Periodicals

Asian Survey (San Francisco).
Commerce (Bombay).
Current Digest of the Soviet Press (New York).
Economic and Political Weekly (Bombay).
India and Foreign Review (New Delhi).
International Studies (Bombay).
Link (New Delhi).
Mizan (London).
Pakistan Horizon (Karachi).
Seminar (New Delhi).
Survey (London).
The Statesman's Weekly (New Delhi).
Times of India (Bombay).
Thought (New Delhi).

INDEX

121